M000195553

Nathalie Michelle
Deep Waters
Trusting God When Your Feet Can't Touch Bottom
Printed in the United States of America

KUDU

Deep Waters:

Trusting God When Your Feet Can't Touch Bottom

By: Nathalie Michelle

Table of Contents

Dedication   7

Acknowledgements   9

Foreword   13

SECTION I: IMMERSED   **19**

Chapter 1   Shipwrecked   21

Chapter 2   Still Waters   29

Chapter 3   Riptide   43

Chapter 4   S.O.S.   65

SECTION II: SUBMERGED   **81**

Chapter 5   Into the Deep   83

Chapter 6   Finding Your Lighthouse   93

Chapter 7   Swimming Lessons   107

Chapter 8   An Anchor in the Storm   127

SECTION III: EMERGING   **137**

Chapter 9   Treading Water   139

Chapter 10   A New Destination   147

Chapter 11   Returning to Shore   161

Chapter 12   My Safe Harbor   169

Notes   177

DEDICATION

Brandon, I dedicate this book to you;

for without you, there would be no story.

Thank you for showing me firsthand how to trust God

through the deep waters of this life.

ACKNOWLEDGEMENTS

To my Lord and Savior Jesus Christ, our walk has been unlike any other. You gave me this story, and I believe You will use it for Your glory. I am eternally grateful for Your love, provision and hand upon my life. "You sent from above, You took me; You drew me out of many waters." Psalm 18:16

To Mama and Tatie, the women I aspire to emulate: Thank you for showing me what true faith is. Thank you for introducing me to the Love of my life at such an early age. Your sacrifices have not been in vain. You taught me how to be strong and virtuous. You walked with me through every step of this journey; my gratitude knows no bounds. I pray only God's best upon you. I love you.

To my girls: Best friend, patos locos forever, sisters, ma cocotte, amigas, bosom buddies, aunties, friends for life. I cherish each of you. I treasure the imprint you've made on my life. You stood by my side on the happiest day of my life and then beyond, on the day that started this book. You let me vent. You held me as I cried and questioned God. You inspired me. You pushed me; you prayed with me. I am who I am now because you're in my life. I love you all.

To the girl in the khaki dress…Your wisdom, wit, and unconditional friendship made us lifelong Spelman sisters that day. I love you to the moon and back again. I'm forever grateful for you. Thank you for always letting me talk it out. Here's to decades more of Paris days and Cancun nights (minus you know what).

To the men in my life: Pastors, fathers, brothers, cousins, and friends. Where would I be without you? Your wisdom, spiritual covering, laughter, friendship, and unconditional support have made me the woman I am today. Thank you for allowing God to use you in such a major way in my life.

To Bishop Daddy Eddie L. Long and First Lady Vanessa Long and my New Birth family: Thank you for your leadership, wisdom and support. Your obedience to the Lord and adherence to His word -no matter the cost- set the tone for my journey. I am forever grateful.

To the Coward family: Thank you for raising the man that changed my life forever. His impact on my life and others will always be felt.

Ma famille française: Merci pour notre belle aventure qui m'a montrée une nouvelle façon de regarder la vie. J'aurai toujours dans ma memoire les leçons apprises et les souvenirs que nous avons partagés ensemble.

Je vous aime tant.

To new acquaintances: I've met through the waves of this deep water experience and beyond. Our random encounters on airplanes, nail salons, networking events, and elsewhere have made this dream become a reality for me. Thank you for wanting to read this story, I hope it enriches your life and encourages you to live on top!

Foreword

I never thought there could be so much healing in remembering pain. But there is something to be said for the beauty of brokenness...

When I was younger, I used to get distracted by churches' stained-glass windows. Too young to be intrigued beyond the singing part of the service, once the choir sat down, I found myself lost in a world of colors and light. They became my sermons as I would stare off and marvel at how these pieces of broken, colorful glass could come together to tell such a beautiful story. I wondered if those individual pieces were discarded for their brokenness. Instead, someone saw the value and potential in each one and made something truly captivating out of them. Such is the case with my friend Nathalie and the pieces that make up her story. The same can be said for so many of us...

Broken by life experiences, people let us down. Our expectations haven't been met; our trust has been betrayed. Things just didn't go quite as planned. These are the elements of our brokenness. Viewed individually, they are simply shards of past, painful memories we hope to soon forget. But artfully combined, they come together in kaleidoscopic brilliance. Ultimately, no matter how beautiful it is, it isn't until a bright light shines through that stained glass truly becomes magnificent.

My best friend's story, this story you hold in your hands, is just one example of the pieces coming together. Through the pages that follow, Nathalie documents her journey to brokenness and back again. She chose to write and share her story with you. In so doing, she is bravely letting her light shine through her own brokenness. And it is beautiful. But the real beauty comes from knowing that brokenness is not where the story ends. When Nathalie pledged her allegiance to the man she loved on her wedding day, how could she have known the time between "from this day forward...'till death do us part" was only going to be 502 days; the equivalent of less than a year and a half? And if she had known, would she have done anything differently?

The Christian model of marriage reflects the husband as a "covering" for his wife (and family). When Nathalie's life was abruptly interrupted, she lost her "covering" and essentially her sense of security. **But God...** God sent His Holy Spirit to be everything a covering represents. He shielded her, protected her and gave her sanctuary. Yes, this is a story of heartache and loss. But it is also a story of restoration and healing. It is an intimate look into what happens beyond the five hundred and second day; beyond the pain, beyond the heartache, beyond the frustration, and beyond the struggle.

This book is an expression of faith and a demonstration of true bravery. Knowing how painful it was for me with each turn of the page, I had to wonder how painful it was for her with each stroke of her pen. I knew the story already, so it surprised me how many times I cried. But when I think of it, my tears were more deeply rooted than simply remembering a "rough patch" in the past. I cried tears of gratitude, joy and pride as I read my sister's words and saw the manifestation of her growth on these pages. The charge to "rejoice with those who rejoice [and] mourn with those who mourn" in Romans 12:15 is one that I take fiercely to heart. I do this not just because the Bible commands it; it's just how God made me. I consider it a privilege to share in the joys and sorrows of the people I hold dear. And Nathalie is someone I hold dear.

The vast majority of you probably didn't know the slick talking, nameplate-wearing, Haitian girl from Hollis, Queens that I once knew. She is someone who, in all her stubbornness, refused to call me by my actual name, but rather by a name she chose for me based on what she *thought* it should be. I never could have imagined I'd become best and lifelong friends with the same girl who didn't find that particular detail to be of much importance. But I did. She has come a long way from being that girl. A woman now, she has blossomed beautifully. I am certain that the man who loved her for who she was then is smiling down in amazement at who she has become now. The Bible says "a man that finds a wife finds a good thing." When Brandon T. Coward got to Morehouse College, he truly did find a good thing. Today, I step back in awe and marvel at how a "good thing" can become an even greater thing...

You don't have to read Nathalie's story to know that a lot can change in a year (for better or for worse). Through it all, regardless of which way the pendulum swings; cling to those closest to you, embrace the process, and never discard your broken pieces. Let God put the pieces back together and make something lovely. These are usually the pages everyone skips over. But if you're still reading, then these words were intended especially for you. I don't have to know why you picked up this book; I'm just glad you did. You may not even know the reason... But hopefully you will by the time your eyes grace the final page. For me, reading her story makes me want to be closer to Christ. If nothing else, I pray it does the same for you.

Courtney Sabra Marie
> *"...and so, having patiently waited, he obtained the promise."*
> *(Hebrews 6:15)*

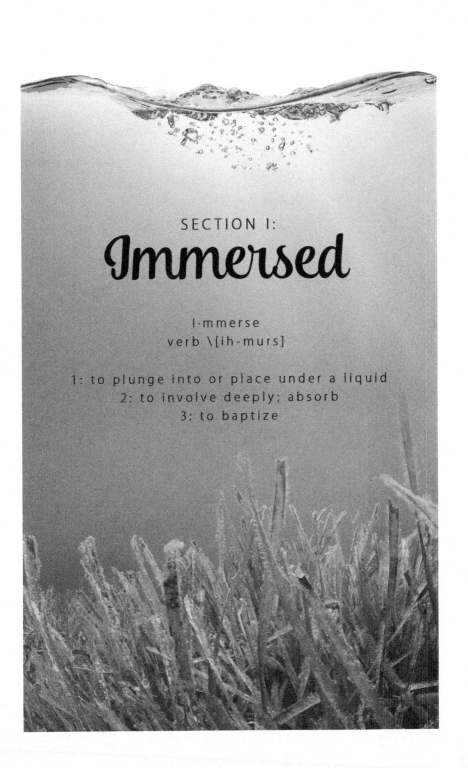

SECTION I:

Immersed

I·mmerse
verb \[ih-murs]

1: to plunge into or place under a liquid
2: to involve deeply; absorb
3: to baptize

Chapter 1:

Shipwrecked

E yes shut, breath fighting against the barrier I was forced to create with my pursed lips, my flailing arms struggled to grab on to anything, something I could hold on to. My legs felt like anchors, pulling me to the bottom. I wildly turned my head around in an effort to find my rescuer, but all I saw was the rapidly growing darkness of the ocean depths. Terrified, I fought my death, but why? In one foul moment, I was violently thrust overboard the ship headed towards "Happily Ever After," when a storm called Ripped destroyed my happiness and wrenched true love out of my embrace. My heart was torn to pieces, as the one whom my soul loved died in the arms of strangers one cold January night. I lost everything in a violent tragedy that bloodied the scene and wounded my heart simultaneously. Battered, I relinquished my will to live and sunk further into the abyss of sorrow-filled waves.

The rhythmic underwater current belied the death grip I was trapped by. Eventually, I was lulled to my final sleep. As the woeful nothingness filled my senses, I died to myself, and my plan for happiness. I lost my blueprint for perfection and a life that mirrored a fairytale.

I was completely undone.

Balled up fists beating on my chest snatched me out of my watery grave. Life-giving oxygen filled my lungs as I involuntarily gasped and coughed up the remains of my end. Angry tears flooded my face as I slowly opened them to see the sky again. My fate was changed in those repeated, angry assaults on my heart. I had to breath again. I had to live again. My invisible Rescuer had now made me the sole survivor and the wreckage was horrifying.

Where do I go from here? How can any of this ever look "normal" again? As the certainty of my pain set in, I had a choice to make: die in the depths or live on top.

I chose the latter, but it would not be easy. In the aftermath of my storm, I searched for answers in the deep waters of grief, sorrow, and brokenness. Everything that could be affected was shaken. My faith in true love, lasting happiness, and even God Himself was challenged in ways that I could not have prepared for. What happened to my faith? Was I being punished? Can Bible verses of hope and love, like the ones you see plastered on bumper stickers and t-shirts, really help in moments like that? Can you still sing the songs of how wonderful or great God is and really mean it?

There is a popular saying that goes something like this: *if you want to make God laugh, tell Him your plans.* I guess He was rolling over and wiping the tears from His eyes when, years ago, I painted a picture of the safe life I believed I was destined to have. I always wanted a "normal" life like the one you see on television. I wanted a mom and a dad that made perfectly timed comedic remarks throughout my teenage soliloquies. I asked Him for a cute boyfriend that would transform high school into an exciting, coming-of-age saga that would teach me lessons. I wanted all this to eventually lead into a college spin-off that taught me what real life was all about. All this would happen while I relied on the financial support of my parents until I was ready to step out on my own. Of course, all of this would be done while wearing the latest fashions and trends. My prayer was not answered, but what He produced was far greater than anything I could ever come up with on my own.

I have tried to be content in whatever depths I might find myself in, but in all honesty, I oftentimes fail. Anyone can be happy during the joyous times of this journey, when we are cruising on the serene waters of weddings, birthdays, graduations, promotions, good health, new babies and new cars. These are all wonderful times to celebrate and be happy.

But how do we stay afloat in the raging tempests of divorce, betrayal, infertility, financial ruin, abuse, negative doctor's reports, lost opportunities and death? The panic of not being able to see clearly into the depths becomes the perfect breeding ground for fear and self-pity.

The biblical apostle James tells us that we should "... *count it all joy when you fall into various trials, knowing that the testing of your faith produces patience. But let patience have its perfect work, that you may be perfect and complete, lacking nothing.*"[1] Despite all of his hardship and trials, the apostle Paul said "*I think myself happy.*"[2] When Jesus faced the mammoth of all trials, he submitted to God and prayed, "*My Father, if it is possible, may this cup be taken from me. Yet not as I will, but as you will.*"[3]

These verses should have comforted me, right? What about you? These verses and others like them should be just the thing that one needs in the face of difficult trials, but what if they don't help like you think they should?

Now, before you close this book, I challenge you to be real with yourself and with God. Have you ever experienced a gut-wrenching pain that engulfed your life, family, career, or health? Have you ever felt like you were drowning and no one could save you? You scream for help, but it seems that no one can hear you. You reach out, but you're only met with clichés and awkward reassurances. Have you ever prayed and cried out for God to intervene or reverse a negative situation and felt like things only got worse? Let me be real. I have! The Bible is full of direct scriptural examples of how we should react when we face terrible times. God's word doesn't just paint pretty pictures of blessings and joy. He depicts real men and women that had their plans seized from them. They experienced deep waters of loneliness, death, frustration, debilitating pain, impossible odds and promises that weren't always fulfilled in expected timetables.

Odd as it may seem, discomfort and pain reinforce our faith walk as they directly force us to face ourselves. Tragic circumstances make us more aware of our temporary existence and often lead us to either move forward from our painful interruption, stand still or move backwards towards the comfort of our life before the pain.

What about your life? What about your unique circumstance? What was your reaction to the painful interruption that caused you to lose your footing and grip on life?

I can only speak from my own experience, but I want to illustrate a story of hope that I pray penetrates past your deepest affliction. I warn you, this trip won't be easy. In fact, it has been the hardest thing I've ever undergone. I know that everyone's journey is different, but my hope is that you are able to find something here that will strengthen you to continue living despite the seeming impossibility that surrounds you. I believe there is a reason that you picked up this book, and there is something uniquely hidden within its pages for you.

The following chapters of this book are divided up into sections that parallel some of my life circumstances. These symbolic divisions capture various moments of contact with life's deep waters. I've included actual journal entries to be as honest and raw as possible.

Throughout this book, I will make references to Jesus Christ and will include biblical stories along with Scripture to support certain topics. Please do not let that stop you from being able to relate. Pain is pain, and you don't have to be a Bible scholar or a Christian to understand that. I have chosen to rely on my faith to traverse the waters of difficulty that I have experienced, and at times I may include instructions for a personal growth activity or an invitation to pray. At all times, please do as you feel led. Above all, I am honored to be sharing such a personal story with you. I value your time, so let's not waste another moment and begin.

Let's get back on the ship that was headed towards *Happy*...ready?

Chapter 2:

Still Waters

Y ou know that feeling of pure happiness and joy that threatens to burst through every pore of your body? Do you know that feeling of pure euphoria, making your cheeks hurt from smiling too much? If you could fly, you would. You giggle and stare off into space as you contemplate how fortunate and blessed you are. You may hum to yourself or even sing and dance around. Your happiness knows no bounds; it may even be contagious. That moment was happening for me today, September 15, 2007. It was finally here! I have dreamed of this moment for as long as I could remember.

I had planned it over and over again in my head, yet countless subscriptions to wedding magazines, daily visits to *theknot.com* and binge watching *A Wedding Story* paled in comparison to the feeling I now felt. Nothing that I had imagined or visualized equaled the beauty of the actual moment. Everything sparkled. It was as if time stood still to bring to attention that today was my wedding day. This was the day I was going to marry my man!

I tried to sleep the night before, but to no avail. The night was filled with such excitement and energy. A bubble fiasco almost destroyed my wedding dress as my maid of honor and I had the bright idea of trying to use the bath steam to loosen a few wrinkles that the seamstress had forgotten. Courtney and I temporarily forgot about it while we were chatting about the big day ahead...bad idea. When we finally realized what was happening, we had an overflowing mess of bubbles and steam in the bathroom. But thankfully, the dress was saved! We promptly went to bed to get some rest before the morning.

As I lay awake on my big day, I remembered the rain the night before, so I got out of bed and looked out the window. I held my breath as I pulled back the curtains. I couldn't believe my eyes! A misty fog covered the ground outside. Of all the days to have rain and humidity... "What would my hair look like?!" I thought. My girls rushed to my rescue by quickly reminding me of the beauty of the occasion and encouraging me to stay in the moment (and not become a bridezilla), persuading me to not worry about things outside my control. So instead, I chose to focus on this my favorite month, September. I remembered the newness I always attributed to this month. It reminded me of all my first days of the school year, new school clothes and shoes, as well as my maturation into the next stages of my life.

This September was by far the most important marker. It would literally be the cake-topper on my slice of elation. Despite the threat of rain, my bridesmaids and I continued getting ready for my big moment. My stylist swept my hair up in an elegant up-do and used her tools to give me a "fresh face look," You know, the one that makes it look like you have no make up on? It took an hour, but it was well worth it. My nails and eyebrows were perfectly manicured and arched. I sprayed my favorite perfume on my wrists, collarbone and behind my ears. I was so nervous and happy that I could hardly eat the breakfast one of my bridesmaids graciously ordered for me. I could not wait for everything to get started! But I almost forgot, I had to send my beloved his wedding present. I had purchased and engraved a money clip to hold all of his loose bills. My maid of honor took it down to the men's suite and returned with a letter on hotel stationery. I laughed, as I knew this meant he had forgotten his present for me. Nonetheless, I cherished his words of love and excitement about our upcoming nuptials.

One of my bridesmaids helped me to fasten beautiful pearls around my neck, a gift from my mother on my sixteenth birthday. My mother and aunts stepped in to lace up my corset and make sure everything was picture-perfect ready as the photographer tried to capture each moment on film. Some of the most important ladies in my life joined hands with me as my beautiful maid of honor gave thanks and praise to the Father, asking for His blessings on this special day. We bowed our heads, stood in a circle and prayed. This day felt as if God was actively pouring out His happiness and lavishing all I loved with His grace.

"In Jesus' name, Amen."

My mother gracefully pulled the veil over my face as I readied myself to walk down the aisle to marry Brandon T. Coward. I was so ready to join with him. The four years of our courtship had finally brought us to this longed-for moment.

A thin curtain of sheer lace separated me from the ceremony. As I waited for my turn down the aisle, my mind raced with images and scenes of our romance: I saw the day I first noticed him on the church shuttle bus back in college. He looked so sophisticated and mature. His New York accent echoed through the bus as he bowed his curly head to ask the Lord for traveling mercy on our way to church. I remembered being captivated by his style, yet determined to not let him know. It was more than difficult; all I knew was that I wanted him. As bold as that seems, in my innocence, I could not articulate it past that. I saw our first conversation, which was, ironically, an argument. It took place at a college ministry trip, and we were arguing over whether New York or Atlanta would be the ideal place to live after graduation. He was determined to adapt to Atlanta, while I couldn't wait to get back to "the city that never sleeps".

The images fast-forwarded to our first date, which was actually a first for both of us. I never dated before because, honestly, I was terrified of getting hurt. I never wanted the vulnerability of being in love with someone. I did not want a broken heart. I had watched enough TV sitcoms and listened to enough friends to decide that relationships and love just weren't worth the pain they could cause. I did not want to deal with the emotional baggage that a broken heart brought with it. The risk involved in trusting someone else and becoming vulnerable is not appealing. In romantic comedies, the misguided couple often face seemingly random difficulties, which we laugh and poke fun at. When in truth, we fear the reality of our own relationships. The veracity of my own fears in relationships almost made me miss my opportunity at experiencing true love. God had other plans. Nonetheless, I stayed focused on my goals of success and locked my heart away until one day, God overhauled my plans. He shared the key with the one assigned to love me and me alone.

November 2003

O God, my Father, I don't know what to do. I don't even know how to describe how I feel... Lord, You see how much it takes for me to even begin to conceive of letting someone in... I hate, absolutely abhor feeling vulnerable. I have other things to think about: class registration, financial aid, books for my major, studying abroad, my plane tickets home, my family, my grades- but then I keep hearing You say: don't think on these things, and be still, know that I AM God.

But Father, let me know, have I awakened and stirred up love too soon? Am I naïve? Speak to me Lord.

In Jesus' name I pray,
Amen and Amen

It's hard to describe, but there truly was something different about him, something that made him stand out amongst all the rest. So when he asked me out to our colleges' joint homecoming ball, I said "yes," and the rest was quite literally...history.

November 2003

O Lord, what a night! I still can't believe that I'm actually 19! The dance was wonderful, Brandon, a Godsend, and my night, absolutely lovely. Well, interest has been acknowledged openly between Brandon and I. . . .I pray that You remain the center, source, and focus on and of our lives. You've begun a great work, and I will continue to trust and abide in You.

In Jesus' name,

Amen

From that moment on, we began courting. We made a promise to God and each other to keep our virginity until we were married. It was not easy, but the day we had both vowed to wait for had finally arrived! At dinner, I beamed with joy as I played out the scene of him proposing to me on our graduation night. Surrounded by my family, he asked me to be his wife, his partner and his happily ever after; and my answer had brought us to this day.

> *May 14, 2006*
>
> *He proposed to me! Lord this day has been so blessed! Jesus, I need You to know how grateful I am. I have successfully completed my education at Spelman College and today my Morehouse man asked me to marry him!!! The feelings I have are of awe and surprise. I am so honored and blessed to have been chosen by Brandon. You have put into place a wonderful new beginning for me. The best is yet to come.*
>
> *Thank you Father!*

I was so lost in my reverie that I almost didn't notice the sun had finally burst forth from behind the clouds as I made my way down the aisle. He beamed with pride as he met my gaze. He later told me that I took his breath away as he realized that this day wasn't just a dream anymore. A solitary tear streamed down his face as he looked at me, his bride. The ceremony was a blur; I just kept waiting for my cue. I tried to make a conscious effort to take mental photos in order to forever engrave them in my memory bank. I tried to soak up every laugh, look and well-wisher. I wanted to savor every moment; I did not want to forget a thing.

When it was my turn, I repeated my vows from our college minister, meaning every word:

I, Nathalie, take you Brandon, to be my husband, to have and to hold from this day forward, for better or for worse, for richer, for poorer, in sickness and in health, to love and to cherish; from this day forward until death do us part.[4]

We sealed our covenant with a kiss and held hands as we were introduced for the first time as Mr. and Mrs. Brandon Coward. I was so happy! Married life would finally start for me, and I could not wait. I looked into the sea of faces, comprised of friends and family who had traveled from all over to celebrate with us on this joyous day. The reception continued the festivities. The toasts and dances were fun and memorable. The videographer captured friends and family as they let loose to celebrate with us. We laughed, reminisced and shared our gratitude with those we loved. I threw my bouquet and laughed with my single friends who hoped to be the next to skip into wedded bliss. My heart burst with joy each time I looked at my new husband. We were official! We had waited for each other, and we couldn't wait to start our new lives together.

We went through that awkward first dance and posed for what seemed like a million and one "perfect" photos. He firmly placed his hands over mine as we cut into the tower of confectionary goodness. We had an arrangement, therefore cake only made it into my mouth, not on my face. The DJ set the atmosphere for Brandon to go under my dress and...retrieve the garter. Unlike the ladies before, the men were in no rush to catch it and follow in my new husband's footsteps. The minutes flew by, and as our celebration drew to a close, we reveled in the bittersweet moments as we waved goodbye to our former selves and childlike innocence, and welcomed everything that married life had to offer... And I do mean *everything*! While I thoroughly enjoyed being surrounded by family and friends, I couldn't wait to be alone with my husband, just him and me. In those special moments when we were alone together, I caught a glimpse of true love. I never wanted to look away.

After our honeymoon in Jamaica, life took on a rhythm that we were quickly able to adjust to. As pleasant and idyllic as that sounded, there were some major adjustments that we needed to make. I went from being a single college girl to living with a man who didn't see any problem with leaving his smelly gym clothes on the floor or the toilet seat up (not cool in the middle of the night!). He fussed at my annoying habit of buying brand name and organic food items instead of the ones on sale. I nicknamed him Brandon "Budget" Coward as he tried to curb my single-girl spending tendencies. We had recently purchased a house, and we were excited to make it our home. I couldn't wait to go shopping; he couldn't wait to tell me what I couldn't buy. Although we had a different way of doing things, such as how to arrange our living room furniture, compromise became a cornerstone of our marriage. I had to learn that it didn't mean one person does what *I* want. Daily, we would look at all we had been blessed with and thank God for His unmerited grace and favor on two kids from the projects of New York City.

We had brand new careers to match the freshness of our life together. He was a financial analyst, and I was a first grade teacher. Our life was as perfect as it could get. I had worked my plan and succeeded. I thought "This is how the Lord blesses those whom He loves!" I just knew God was proud and that the happiness we shared daily was evidence of that. We were learning what "cleaving" meant and looked forward to celebrating each wedding anniversary. Life wasn't perfect, but we just knew that we could overcome anything as long as we had each other. When rocky moments did come, such as a downsizing at Brandon's job and the sudden passing of my aunt and grandmother, we held onto each other. With each new occurrence, we would adjust our spreadsheets and continue planning for our future.

2008

Papa,

Had it not been for You and Your grace, I know that I would not have made it. You are so loving, so kind, and good. Jesus as Your word says, unless You had been my help, my soul had almost dwelt in silence. This past year, You've stretched me and pushed me out of my comfort zone. Your strength has enabled me to be where I am today. I take nothing for granted in our relationship together. Jesus, guide my marriage. Lead my husband, the man You've entrusted me to. Show him where he should go. Help him to be sensitive to my needs and desires and help me to be accommodating and giving. I love him and trust him because of You. Let our love never grow old, but let it flourish and mature into an even stronger bond. Guide us and help us to be strong and to make wise decisions Holy Spirit. May Your will be done Jesus.

In Jesus' name,

Amen

Brandon began studying for the GMAT with the intentions of going to business school, and I began my pursuit of a Master's Degree in teaching. The economic market had just begun its slump; gas prices were on the rise, and even teaching was no longer a guaranteed career path. However, as life continued to throw its curve balls, we determined to align ourselves accordingly. Adversity often has a way of causing you to question your foundation. Hard times force you to look to your source of strength. We were determined to still trust in God, despite what we saw with our eyes or heard on the news.

We celebrated our first wedding anniversary towards the end of 2008. Brandon surprised me with a weekend trip to Panama City, Florida. We had a blissful time of romance and great food. I wanted to start a family, but Brandon thought it wiser to start off with a puppy. He promised to get me one soon.

We prayed and sought to strengthen our personal relationships with Christ. We continued to be stretched beyond our limits at varying points. Those were the moments we had to turn our faith to our limitless God. Looking back, all of those events were opportunities to grow in our faith. It was never easy, but I always felt that anything was possible as long as I had God and my husband. I never allowed myself to think about a life without him. After all, why should I?

Chapter 3:

Riptide

As the ball dropped in Times Square and the Peach made its way down at Underground Atlanta, January 2009 brought with it a fresh new canvas of opportunity and experience. My journal entry captures my excitement and readiness to begin a new year:

January 1, 2009

Lord,

You are my shepherd and I shall not want. You lead me and guide me. I will not lean on my own understanding but trust in You always! I'm excited to live this year according to Your standards, system, and structure. I yield to You and approach this new year with childlike faith as I seek You first and keep my eyes and faith stayed on You. Be God this year and always. Show me step by step where You want me Lord and how You want me to get there. Blindfold me in Your Spirit and lead me down Your path. Revolutionize my bloodline, this nation, and this world. Do a new thing and now let it spring forth!

In Your Son and Spirit,

Amen

Fresh new calendars and planners filled our household as we prepared for another year together. By this time, I had begun to "master" the routine of my roles as teacher, student and wife. A typical day consisted of teaching and entertaining 22 first graders, attending one of three graduate courses and then driving for about 45 minutes back home in unprecedented Atlanta traffic. It was a grueling schedule, yet we still sought to make time for one another. I learned to savor the precious moments I was able to share with my husband. His support and partnership really made those days bearable and even enjoyable. I loved being married! Daily, I was afforded the opportunity to get to know him on a level that I had never shared with anyone.

To accommodate for our busy schedules and dwindling "us time," Brandon would often wake up early, prepare my breakfast and then surprise me by driving me to work. Those morning drives were an excellent way to increase our intimacy and deepen our connection. We were still in the honeymoon stage of our marriage and tried to prolong it as much as possible. Sometimes I would just lay my head on his shoulder, enjoying his presence. Other times, we would engage in discussions ranging from the very deep to the funny and lighthearted. More than anything, I just loved being able to just sit back and ride.

This arrangement actually worked out perfectly because in late January, my car needed servicing and was in the shop. For almost a full week, Brandon drove me to work and picked me up from graduate school. On a Wednesday morning, he dropped me off with a kiss and a hug; we made arrangements for him to pick me up from a friend's place after my class since he had a meeting to attend at church later that evening.

Right before class started, I called Brandon to check on him and make sure we were still on schedule.

"Hey baby. I'm about to head into class. Don't forget to pick me up..."
"Baby, how could I forget? I love you."
"I know...I know... I was just playing around. So do you want me to give the directions to the apartment now or do you just want to call me?"
"I don't want to make you late for class, so I'll call you when I leave church."
"Ok. I love you. See you later."
"I love you too baby. See you later."

The minutes actually moved along pretty quickly as I tried my best to remain engaged in my math class. It was over a little early, at around 7:30 p.m. My girlfriend and I met another friend and got some dinner together with music and movies; we had the perfect recipe for a fun girls' night. We settled in and began enjoying a night of girl-talk and laughter. I was having so much fun that I didn't realize the time was getting late and that I had still not heard from Brandon. Around 9:00 p.m., I called Brandon's phone to give him directions to the apartment. His phone went to voicemail immediately, so I left a message. Thirty minutes later, I still heard nothing from him. I called again and sent a text message, all to no avail. I started to feel a little worried because this was not like him at all. Finally, in desperation I sent him an email, hoping it would go through on his Blackberry.

Babe, I'm really scared right now, where are you? I've called you and called you and texted you...still nothing. I've called the house phone and nothing. Please I pray that the Lord has kept you safe....call me or text me ...I am going to get a ride home... Please call me when you get this email. I love you forever.

Ten minutes or so later, I had still received no response. I began to allow myself to fear the worst. I fought it desperately. It felt like I was drowning. Swirling thoughts of the worst possible outcomes attacked my mind like an unpredicted blizzard. Suddenly, I remembered one of our friends would be in attendance at the same meeting, so I called his wife.

"Hey honey, I was just calling to see if you had heard from Joe yet. I've been calling Brandon and his phone just keeps going to voicemail."
"Really? Well Joe's been home for a little while now. Wait, let me ask him if he spoke to Brandon."
Joe's voice in the background, told me what I didn't want to hear, *"You know, come to think of it, I don't remember seeing him at the meeting."*
"He wasn't at the meeting?!"

That was over 2 hours ago! My heart began beating rapidly in my chest. I tried to think rationally. I said a quick prayer and then updated my two friends. They tried to reassure me that everything was okay and that maybe Brandon's phone had run out of battery. Maybe, he was trying to figure out a way to get to me, since I hadn't given him the directions yet. None of those explanations made sense, but I had to hold onto something as the reality of the situation threatened to overwhelm me again.

"Why isn't he calling me back? Where is he? Oh God, please protect him. Keep him safe. When I see him, he's going to be in so much trouble, making me worry like this! Jesus, please, please, bring me to him."

The only plan of action was to drive to my house. My girlfriends tried to make conversation and get my mind away from the path of thoughts it was currently on. I remember listening to music but not hearing the lyrics. That drive home was the longest I had ever taken. When we pulled up to the house, a lonely light was seen from the window. *He was home! Thank God! I couldn't wait to hear his explanation!* I entered through the garage and walked inside; the stillness inside suffocated me. His car wasn't there. My friends ran inside to identify the source of the light: he had accidentally left the office light on upstairs. My legs weakly took me around our kitchen, our living room, looking for a sign from him, something from him. Anything from him. Suddenly, I noticed the red, blinking light from our answering machine. I skipped past telemarketers and empty silence to finally land on a message from the local hospital.

"Brandon Coward was in a car accident. Please call immediately."

Relief hit me. At least I knew where he was, but the reality of what may have occurred made my heart hit the floor. Like a robot, I grabbed my phone and dialed. After explaining who I was and the message I had received, I was transferred to the nurse on duty. She covered the phone loosely with her hand, whispered something to someone near her, and then told me she was transferring me again.

"I'm looking for my husband, Brandon Coward. I received a message that he was in an accident. Can you please tell me what room he's in? I can be there very soon."
"Yes, please hold just a moment. I have to transfer you to the nurse in triage."

My thoughts were on fire! What's taking so long? I thought of so many possible scenarios. *What if he was unconscious...well of course that's why he never answered my calls! Oh God, but what if he was a quadriplegic? I still love him Lord! I do! It will be hard, but we can make it with You.*
"Mrs. Coward? Mrs. Coward?" The nurse's voice on the phone snatched me out of the raging rivers of my thoughts.
"Yes. I'm here."
"Mrs. Coward is someone with you?"

Why did this matter? Why didn't she just tell me what room he was in so I could go to him?

"Yes. What's going on?"
"Honey, I'm sorry, but he had a lot of internal bleeding...we tried....we couldn't stop it... he was declared dead shortly after his arrival...."

"What! What time? How do you know it was him?!" I yelled my inquiries to her as I struggled to understand what sounded like a foreign language to me.

"I'm so sorry. It was around 7:30 p.m. We tried calling you, but due to the severity of the crash, we could only use the number listed on his driver's license...your house phone."

That was 3 hours ago!
"But, how do you know it was him?" My questions bordered on the verge of hysteria; my friends who by this time realized something major had happened, moved in closer.

"Well honey, there's a wedding photo with your name on the back, his name is listed as..."

I swiftly interrupted her, *"can I come see him tonight, please?"*
I begged.

"I don't know how to say this, but he's already been transferred to the city morgue, which is closed now, and besides his body can only be released to a funeral home."

His body? My mind wanted to explode.

Immediately, I was on the ground. One of my friends took the phone from me. I curled up into a tight ball and covered my face and head with my hands. It was as if I were trying to shut out the pain that suddenly blanketed me. In the distance, I heard my friend's voice as she verified and wrote down the name of the morgue where my husband's lifeless body lay. There wouldn't be time for a final goodbye. I couldn't breathe. I needed this to be the worst nightmare. I wanted to wake up. I instantly thought about the spaghetti dinner I had made and were looking forward to sharing.

It was a special, random request from him. Now he wouldn't be here to eat it with me. My next thought was of our love and intimacy; no longer would we be able to kiss and cuddle. The man I had waited on for so long would no longer walk through the door, hold me and share his love with me. Was this what I had waited, prayed and sacrificed for? My heart hurt so badly. I felt as if I had been ripped into unrecognizable shreds.

As I lay in the fetal position on my rug, I rocked back and forth. Suddenly, the unexpected happened; I was drenched in peace. Honestly, it was as if God Himself wrapped His loving arms around me and squeezed. He never let go. I wrestled with Him. I fought with Him. He wouldn't let go. I could not believe that He had allowed this to happen. He knew all along. Why did He let me fall in love? I wanted to scream and be furious with Him. I wanted to hate Him, but I couldn't. It was strange. My inner self still loved Him, but my outside shell fought that idea. I was angry, but I needed Him now more than ever.

As tears flooded my face, the sudden realization that I needed to call and repeat the saddest words I had ever heard to his mother, his father, my family and our friends brought with it a fresh wave of pain. What would I say? How could I tell them what I still could not believe myself? There is no preparation to make or receive a call like that at

2 a.m., but I had to do it. My girlfriends held me as I called his mother first. He was her baby, the youngest of her seven children. I had to tell her that her baby, *our* baby, was gone. My heart broke afresh as her tears and shrieks of pain carried over the telephone. I heard my father-in-law in the distance as he asked what was going on. I had to repeat the ugliest words I had ever been forced to say aloud again. As I continued calling family members and shared their pain, reality set in. This horrible night had actually happened. Statements of disbelief and piercing pain penetrated the deepest part of me. I called my mother and family last. My mother wanted to get on the plane right away; I told her to wait until arrangements were made...*oh God, funeral arrangements*!

Some of our close friends came right over. They shared the load by using the list of wedding invites to make calls expressing the tragic news, how ironic.

I remember wanting to play the role of a hostess but not being able to move my lips or my feet. I lay on my couch wrapped in a blanket surrounded by my friends. I was exhausted, but I didn't want to go to sleep. I knew that I would miss him coming through our front door. I went upstairs briefly and entered our room. I closed the door behind me. I wanted to keep his memory in and others out. I wanted to scream. I wanted to rush to our bed and pull the covers over my head. Instead, I walked into our bathroom, looked at the upright toilet seat and shook my head. His sink was nice and neat, as usual. I put the seat down, and then called my best friend Courtney. My sobs heightened her awareness that something was terribly wrong. I told her: "*Brandon no está aquí*..." as the realization set in for her, she shared my anguish and cried with me. She made arrangements for the most feasible flight and reassured me that she would be there for me. I can't remember if I called my other best friends or if someone had already notified them, but through the night, I knew I was not alone.

I stepped back into our bedroom. I smelled his pillow; his manly smell brought instant tears to my eyes. I crawled over to our closet and wrapped myself in his big, blue bathrobe, my first Christmas present to him. I wept from my core into his bathrobe; I tried to keep my voice muffled...I couldn't let go just yet because my friends waited for me downstairs. I looked through our closet and was immediately able to tell which outfit he had been wearing on that night. He had always been meticulous. I wept from the deepest part of me.

Everything was different. Nothing looked familiar.

Life as I knew it would never be the same again. The coldness that overtook my consciousness was swift. The smiling wedding pictures that graced the empty fireplace looked back at me as figments of a past that I could never have again. I felt a penetrating iciness creep from my head down to my feet. With it came that harsh torture that I can only liken to the sudden freezing sensation accompanied by eating ice cream too fast; only this headache wasn't going away, and there was no sweet treat to look forward to after the pain. I would never kiss him again. I would never be held in his arms. I would never hear his laugh again. The warmth he had brought to my life was gone, replaced by the coldest feeling of pain I had ever known.

The hated scene of the accident was just around the corner from our home. The police report said he had to swerve suddenly to avoid hitting a car making an illegal U-turn. As a result, he lost control of the car with nothing to stop him but a telephone pole. It had rained a little earlier in the day, but I couldn't remember if it was wet or not. I pictured the helicopter that airlifted him from the scene to the nearest available trauma hospital. They were forced to find another hospital because the first one was full and could not accommodate someone with his injuries. I envisioned the tangled mess his favorite car was probably in. Try as I might, I was not able to picture him. I could not conjure up an image of him that involved him at the scene of the accident. All I could see was his smiling face and gym clothes that he wore when he dropped me off that fateful morning on his way to work out. All I could picture was his loving face as he leaned in to kiss me goodbye for the last time.

January 28, 2009. It had been 502 days, 12,024 hours, 721,440 minutes and 43,286,400 seconds since we first said, "I do." Now, I hated the look of it on my brand new calendar. It taunted me. It was the end of a thing: the shattering of my every temporary happiness and the beginning of a season of loneliness, confusion, shattered faith, and pain, lots and lots of pain.

January 30, 2009

Lord,

What is happening? Father, we had a plan. . . I can't imagine a day let alone a life without my soul mate and friend. I feel like the wind has been knocked from within me. I feel like I'm drowning. Daddy, what are you doing? I trust You, but this doesn't make sense Father. Where do I go from here? Lord, there are many more words in my heart, more than I could possibly write to You. But this one thing I know, that this, the lowest point in my life, I realize that I can only go up from here. I never thought I'd experience pain like this, but even more so, I never thought that I would be healed the way You are healing me. Although, I have tons of questions and I am angry, hurting, and lonely, yet I choose life. I know You are not finished with me yet. You are not done with me yet. Right?

How do you bury something still alive? How do you lay to rest something that had just begun to live? How do you make sense of it all? Where was the script that I was to follow? What was I supposed to do now?

Where was the life raft I needed to get to the other side? How do you go on living? This experience was teaching me that there was no answer. I didn't have the strength to tread these waters.

The days following Brandon's passing were filled with condolences, insurance arguments and casket shopping. I was losing weight rapidly as I had virtually stopped eating. I barely slept. My body was beginning to reflect the emptiness and disrupted routine my life now was.

I cried fresh tears on the way to the funeral home to make the arrangements. I was accompanied by some of the women who had once stood beside me on the happiest day of my life. As we drove, I held my Bible in my lap; holding it close seemed to bring the cherished words of life closer to me in this stark instance of death. As I rearranged it in my hands, a small index card fell out. I recognized it immediately.

A few months before our nuptials, in eager anticipation, Brandon and I had attended a marriage seminar held at our church. The session used the framework of the traditional wedding vows to address the different components of marriage and the commitment involved. Real-life couples shared their experiences facing trust, infidelity, financial woes, sickness, and ultimately death. For the latter portion, we were each given an index card to write our final words to our beloved spouse. I couldn't bring myself to do the assignment correctly and instead, I chose to write my typical words of love and devotion. I knew I would never have to say good-bye, at least not until seventy or eighty years of marital bliss. How wrong I was.

As with everything, Brandon had put forth his best effort, and those words now rested in my trembling hands. As I read them over and over, I couldn't help but feel overwhelmed by an unexplainable peace as I realized that our Lord had penetrated my pain that He cared about my life as I drove to a place of death. He was showing me that nothing had taken Him by surprise, and that He would make provision for all of my needs. He would "feed me" my lines. He was the ultimate director. He held me in those moments as I wept tears of sadness and confusion. Tortured questions bombarded my mind as I kept asking Him: *How can this possibly be in your plan? How will this work out* for my good? What did we do to You? We were on Your side! Can you bring him back please? I **get** "it" now. You're all powerful."

That elusive "it" really didn't exist in my psyche; I just said that in hopes of praying the right words to make my situation change. Perhaps you've done the same. Maybe you're at that point now. I need you to know that you're not in deep water because God is angry with you. Rather, He loves you; and although you may not feel it, He is using every tear you've cried to water every broken dream you've ever had. You may never understand why you've had to experience pain like that. I still don't. I never will. Yet, I know that you have to trust Him through your anguish. He will gently show you that He has made provision for everything that you will encounter on this journey despite what you feel. He is your lifeline. You will not die. I firmly believe that God does not waste our pain or our time.

I now clung to that hope as I sat in the small, cramped office at the funeral home feeling surreal yet facing reality. Without warning, I was given a small plastic baggie that contained the few salvageable items Brandon had on him the night of the accident. A blood stained circle of gold fell out. It took my breath away. It had remained on

his finger since the day I first lovingly put it on. Now, in my
hands, it didn't look or feel the same. The metal felt cold
and lifeless in my hands. It evoked an end rather than a new
beginning.

I took out his wallet and looked at his driver's
license, now splattered with blood and bent out of shape.
The vibrating, intense knot in my chest worked in tandem
with my unbelief that this moment was really happening.
I signed the papers waiving my right to view the physical
remnants of a man that I had pledged my love and life to. I
wanted to remember him the way he was, alive and smiling,
not dead and cold.

In preparation for the funeral services later that
week I shopped for a white dress, only this time, I wasn't
walking down the aisle to marry my love but to say a final
goodbye. I wanted to look good and represent him well. I
found a simple dress that mirrored my new life perfectly,
bright white fading into an uncertain gray and ending in
a harsh black. I put on simple gray pearl studs and a gray
pearl necklace. I cried as my sister friends helped me brush
my hair down before putting on a dull, gray headband.
Gone was the ivory veil which had once covered my face
in innocent joy and anticipation. In its place I put on dark,

round sunglasses. They served two purposes: shielding me from both the sun and the searching, concerned looks from family and friends. Simple black pumps and a white trench coat completed my look.

I selected pictures to be arranged in the memorial slide show to be played on the day of the funeral. Each photo seemed spoke to specific moments of our relationship that now seemed light years ago: our first date, our college years, vacation pictures, engagement pictures, etc. Choosing details such as whether or not to buy two cemetery plots for the price of one and the words for the headstone were moments of sheer pain for me. What did it matter? A new bride didn't belong in a funeral home. I resisted this new role and struggled to understand where I belonged now.

Final preparations were put in place and the day that I never thought I would see came. On February 6, 2009, I followed behind a coffin containing the broken shell of my girlhood dreams and love that I never imagined would be taken. *"The end of a thing is better than its beginning..."* and so began the eulogy taken from Ecclesiastes 7:8. My mind wrestled with that thought. How could the end of my happiness be better than its start? How could sorrow be better than laughter? What did this mean? I grappled with these thoughts as I sat in the front row, just steps away from my beloved. I knew he wasn't here anymore. I knew he was in our Savior's arms, ready for his next assignment; but that didn't make *me* feel better. Everything was broken. Nothing made sense. Now I wondered... would it ever?

Chapter 4:

S.O.S.

What do you do with the broken pieces of your seemingly fragmented life? How do you trust God when you feel like He's the one who caused you your deepest pain? What is life now? What's the point? I battled and wrestled with these questions during my season of loss. I knew who God said He was to me, and I knew who He had always been. Up until this point in my life, I had never really had a reason to doubt His sovereignty. Sure, I had my share of close calls with collegiate financial aid deadlines, mid-term grades and a host of other issues that seemed tantamount to my very existence at one time. But this was something totally different. I had no road map for this journey. I didn't even want to go on this journey.

You see, I had always played it safe. I stayed in the box, colored inside the lines. I believed that as a Christian, if I just stayed on the straight and narrow, then everything had to work out just right. I knew about "trials and tribulations," but I guess I had always thought if I did my very, *very*, best, that I just wouldn't have to suffer through the major stuff. I resisted change and fought process. I tried to keep things "nice and neat."

As a first-generation American and the first to go to college, there was a lot riding on my success. I couldn't afford to not make it. I couldn't mess up and not fulfill my dreams, which had been engrained in me from childhood. I looked at my current surroundings and determined at a young age that I wanted more. I was created for more. I knew that I could not let my place of origin deter me from my destiny. Yet at the crux of the issue was the fact that I didn't like not knowing what came next. Quite honestly, I struggled with letting God be God. I had a tough time letting Him take the lead in my life, especially when I didn't like how things seemed to be turning out.

"I love you. See you later." His last words to me echoed in my head. I needed to see him now! I didn't want to be here without him. I realized God hadn't given me that choice. I remember feeling so lost as to what my next steps should be. Should I sell the house? Move back to New York? What do I do? Whom should I trust? I had no plan. I had no direction. I didn't know where I was going, let alone

where I wanted to go. I wept and screamed inside as I stood rigidly amongst friends and family, shielding my pain from everyone but myself. *"You're still young...you'll find love again." "Is there any chance you could be pregnant?" "Why aren't you crying?"* Statements and questions like these were whispered to me and around me. They stung. No one understood. I clung to God and begged Him to keep His word and uphold me with His hand.

The frigid air of that February afternoon felt good against my face. The weather helped to remind me that I was still alive despite the death I felt within and around me. In an instant, the tragedy and pain that surrounded me, had also forced me to become more alive. As a result my senses were heightened; I grew more sensitive to my surroundings. Colors and hues became reinforced, and voices became louder and clearer. I remember the blinding whiteness of the rose spray that lay across the casket and the whispered voices offering condolences at the cemetery echoed loudly in my head. The deep baritone of his Morehouse College brothers singing the school hymn one last time over his coffin reverberated in my soul.

I kissed the white rose I placed on his casket. Somehow I thought it would reach him. I needed more time, but there was none left. I felt rushed. I was quickly shuffled along in order to make room for others to say goodbye. I had to keep living despite having been forced to say goodbye to the sweetest part of my existence. I wanted to be alone in my grief, but it felt as if all eyes were on me. I yearned to freeze time. I wished I could go back. I wanted this pain to just stop! In those moments, it seemed as if I ate and breathed pain. I couldn't imagine life without him. However, I had to go on. Life still went on. I had to. So do you. You have to make it! You will make it!

There are generations yet unborn counting on your perseverance. Fight the urge to quit. Cry when you need to. Scream. Yell. As you experience this season, allow your pain to work itself out. It won't last forever, and it must yield you something in return. Your pain is necessary for your future. This painful change needed to occur to push you into your tomorrow. It wasn't a punishment. God wasn't sleeping when it happened. In her study of Job, Beth Moore, says "the goal of life is not the absence of pain." We tend to think the opposite; I know I did.

The week following the internment services ushered in Valentine's Day. How timely, just what I needed to "feel better." This day of love and expressing your heart to your significant other was in direct offense to this unwanted season of my life. Nonetheless, flowers and cards from friends and family filled my home. I was so touched by the unexpected show of compassion that it made me realize how taken care of I was. My mother was still in town, and we planned to go out to dinner with a few of my close friends. The night before Valentine's Day, I was wrought with grief and pain. Just last week I buried the one that I would have celebrated this day of love with. I walked slowly throughout the house as I frequently did during bouts of sadness. I quietly tried to envision Brandon and me at happier times in my life before the "Storm." Slowly, I made my way down the staircase and decided to make myself a snack and eat some of the Valentine's Day chocolates my co-workers had sent for me.

While in the kitchen, I had a sudden urge to look through every cabinet; I'm not sure what I was looking for, but I kept looking. Suddenly, I looked up, above my refrigerator at the two small cabinets we never used. Curiosity got the better of me and served as a welcome distraction to the grief that had become my constant companion. I pulled a chair from the dining room, stood on top and opened the cabinet. My heart skipped a beat. Inside the cabinet were 3 pink and red envelopes, Valentine's Day cards! Tenderly, I took the cards and walked over to my living room couch where I looked at each. None of the cards were filled in yet, but from the covers, it was apparent which card was for me. I read Hallmark's rendering of what I took to be my beloved's intended words for me. I read of how much he loved me and how he thought that I was the best thing that ever happened to him. I read of how he looked forward to sharing a lifetime with me. He knew our love would just get better with time. Tears rolled down my face as I wept once more for what could have been.

The remaining two cards were for his mother and mine, respectively. They echoed words of love and admiration for two wonderful women that had impacted his life as well as his desire to share Valentine's greetings with them both. I am not sure how long I sat on that couch, but I held my card to my chest as I rocked back and forth in anguish. He had truly loved me! Although I knew this to be fact before this moment, there was something about finding these cards after the funeral that drove this truth straight to my heart. I missed him so much. "Oh God," I wondered,

"Where do I go from here?"

Going back to work after only two weeks off was an unwelcome yet necessary process. Those past two weeks had been a blur of funeral arrangements, financial rearranging, closet reorganizing and emotional whiplash. There was no early morning drive to look forward to. Packing my lunch wasn't fun alone without playful banter or intimacy. The night before going back to work was filled with tears and questions.

I wrapped myself in his big, blue bathrobe and cradled my Bible in my arms as I sat in our... now, my closet. It felt like the first day of school, except I wasn't excited to meet my new class. I already knew them- I was the one that had changed. I had gone from Mrs. to Ms. in a day, and I was scared to cry in front of my students and co-workers. We still had 4 months before the end of the school year, and I was already counting down. Everything would be different.

I cried until morning and then readied myself to reconnect with my students. I searched the Bible for inspiring moments of faith and courage, asking the Lord to be a protective shield around me. I called my close sister friends and bowed my head as they prayed on my behalf.

February 15, 2009

Daddy,

I've been reading and meditating on Your Psalms and have found great peace and comfort. Psalm 118:17, 18- I will not die but live. You have not given me over to death. You want me to live and be all that You want me to be. Psalm 116:2, You have turned Your ear to me, I will call on You as long as I live. Verse 3 says that when the cords of death entangled me and I was overcome by trouble and sorrow, You delivered me from tears and stumbling in verse 8. Daddy, sustain and maintain me. I'm counting on You to renew and cover me. Father, be with me. Don't leave me now in my time of greatest need. Lord, I cast all my cares on You. I need You to be my Lord, protector, and my husband. I know Brandon is safe with You. Lord, show me a vision of what You would have me to do. I'm desperate for You. Prepare my transition back to school and Mercer (graduate school). Shield me from questions and comments. Guard my heart and mind in You Jesus. I know that I can only transition out of this season with Your guidance and direction. Father, You are welcome to overflow me with grace, peace, joy, fulfillment, purpose, and redemption. I love You Father.

In Jesus' name,

Amen

By morning, I realized it was now or never. Driving past the accident site around the corner from our home was agony. My route to work also took me past the morgue; I remember asking myself: "How much more of this can I take?" I pulled into the school parking lot and said yet another silent prayer. I was nervous to see everyone, but desperate for a change of scenery. Yes, I had missed my students, and I couldn't wait to see them again. I just didn't know if I was ready for everything else being a teacher brought with it. But as an educator, I had to be 100% in the classroom.

When I walked into the classroom, my students bombarded me with hugs, kisses, handmade letters and cards, dozens of wildflowers picked on the way to school and expressions of love as I've never before seen. I was immediately overwhelmed with a total sense of peace. I saw Him that day in my students. God had expressed His continued love for me through these precious children!

However as cute and precious of a moment that was- it was just a moment! Soon my students were back to their rambunctious selves. The next most pressing issue was the day's lunch choice and the feeding of the class goldfish, rather than the matter of Mrs. Coward's "puffy eyes." In fact, I had "puffy eyes" so often, that my students and I developed an understanding: they thought I had a bad headache. As a result, the classroom enjoyed such extended moments of conflict-free quiet time that I thanked both the Lord and my students daily. Teaching my babies while inwardly crying became a fine art. We would frequently have journal time to express our feelings; I found the process to be therapeutic as it also allowed me a few quiet moments to regain my composure throughout the school day and commune with my Savior.

Life slowly began to take on a routine that reintroduced me to habits that I had once shared with Brandon. Driving to church alone, going to the grocery store alone, cooking for one and sleeping alone made me develop an intimacy with my Lord that I had never experienced before. As beautiful as that may sound, I fought it often. We truly are creatures of habit, and I wanted the chance to live out the habits that I had already lovingly developed with my husband. As I wrestled with my desire for my past routine, the Lord was daily showing me what He had known all along: I would make it. I was making it. I have made it!

From those moments on, I was made more aware of every experienced sensation and each moment became carved into the recesses of my mind. I was determined to remember each instance and to never take anything or anyone for granted again. I started to approach each day with a careful delicacy that was not devoid of curiosity and adventure but was filled with a sense of anticipation and urgency. I grew desperate to see how each day would play out. I noted that I tended to take more care with my words, determined to make every word count-never knowing if they would be my last. You never look at anything the same again. Your vision changes; it tends to become sharper and more focused. I was careful to not fall into any patterns; I never wanted life to become predictable again. Of course, that was easier said than done.

The biggest question that arises at a time of painful transition is **"what now?"** All pre-conceived plans are abandoned as you reach for anything that slightly resembles normalcy. As a result, things that seemed important, even essential, are put aside as your life seems to have come to a screeching halt. I was no stranger to this detour. Days after Brandon's death, I grappled with the idea that the vision which God placed in me had died in that fatal car crash as well. What did my life mean now? Where do I go from here?

When you're at the bottom, all you can do is go up. As deep as your pain may be, the many tears you've cried can only serve to become the ocean you will sail upon to new chapters, memories, and hopefully peace. Your pain serves to strengthen the foundation you didn't realize you were standing on. Trust Him. You are not by yourself. Everything you've survived was crucial to the writing of your life's story.

After Brandon died, one of the first steps to my getting back to life and living was realizing that none of this had taken God by surprise. He had already seen my victory even before I realized I was in the battle. He was in complete control, and He was working a plan that in the end would work out for my good and His glory. There were, and still are, many moments where I've felt engulfed by my pain. You may relate. You may feel that there is no hope. Please pray this prayer with me:

What are You doing to me God? Why is my life in the season it's in right now? I feel so lost sometimes. I don't know up from down. Was all of this in Your plan for my life? I am trying to learn what You want me to during this time. I often wonder why my life changed when it did. What was the purpose? Of course I don't have the answers. I find comfort in knowing that even if I never understand fully why things happened the way they did, You know and You are still in control. You care about the smallest details in my life. I rest in the peace You create in my life. Despite it all, I want to maximize each moment and opportunity that You have blessed me with. Please show me how.

In Jesus' name I pray,
Amen

This process of healing has been anything but easy. Even as I sit to write these words, I am still humbled by where I am today in the aftermath of my life's biggest interruptions. I have always been a planner by nature, some would call it a "control freak," but whatever the title, I liked being in the know. I liked checking things off of my checklist of life. Brandon's death not only left that list crumpled and discarded, but also left me with no clear idea of my purpose. Up until his death, I always wanted to be a simple and traditional wife. I desired to raise children who would live to obey and trust the Lord. I wanted to impact my tiny corner of the world through community service, philanthropy and education.

Naturally, I did not necessarily expect life to be perfect. In fact, I knew that whatever "trials and tribulations" came our way would be faced with faith in God, enduring strength and the love that he and I shared. I just never had a plan for facing those "trials and tribulations" without my partner. I never had a chance to come up with the game plan that would prepare me to succeed in the unlikely event of that happening. In hindsight, I never could have come up with a plan to prepare for any of my life's events. God already knows the specific thoughts and plans that He has for me, even when I don't.

Maybe you are in the midst of something that has you crying out to God for even the slightest hint of direction as to what your next steps should be. Maybe your trial is over and now you stand on the battlefield surveying the outcome, wondering how you will ever pick your way through the wreckage and experience happiness or joy again. Perhaps your storm occurred many, many months or years ago, and you still don't feel you have a very clear vision as to what your purpose is. You thought you did and then, life happened. You're now surviving but not living. Come back to life. You are still here for a purpose. Your pain has forced you to focus. Hone in on that one thing that you can work on as you heal and allow pain to take its course. Although things will never be the same again, that does not mean that you will never feel the joy and happiness of your former self. You will, only this time it will be because of new opportunities and moments in your life. Set your eye on the mark. Do everything and anything in faith to press on! I want to encourage you, not only through my own story but also its aftermath. Get to know "you" again. Whatever has happened to you or around you has changed you, but it is not the end of His promise or purpose for you.

February 22, 2009

Lord, I realize that I have come to my end and now You begin. I want to dream again and trust You. You know the thoughts and questions that race through my mind and heart daily. I want to hope for a future in You, it's just that I have no idea what that future looks like and what I should pray for. Can You show me? Can You please cover me and protect me against my raging thoughts? Lord, I don't want to get so deep into my grief that I don't allow room for Your grace; Your grace that I know is sufficient for me. I know You are using me for Your glory. Help me to cope, thrive, and to heal. This season is definitely the lowest and most hurtful that I've experienced; yet at the same time, it is the season that I can learn the most from being directly in Your presence. Help me to not rush through Your process. Remind me that You are not finished with me and that You already know the plans and promises You have for me. . .

In Jesus' name,

Amen

----

[1] James 1: 2-4 NKJV

[2] Acts 26:2a NKJV

[3] Matthew 26:39 NIV

[4] Taken from the Book of Common Prayer

SECTION II:
Submerged

Sub·merge
verb \suh b-murj\

1: to cover; bury
2: to be covered or lost from sight

Chapter 5:

Into the Deep

As the waters slowly began to settle around me, the seeming finality of my circumstance caused an inward need to rediscover who I was and what my new purpose would now be. When I married Brandon, I instantly began to envision my future with him. However, sudden singleness now brought with it a new set of challenges and redirection. I had to reprogram my mind away from the life that I had already lived with him in my head. I searched for books and articles on what a young widow with no children should do. Although I found helpful guides on how to deal with finances, in-laws and the cycles of grief, I still felt that nothing really spoke to my specific needs or situation.

Everything I encountered seemed to be geared towards women who had been married for at least a decade or a young woman who had lost her love to sickness or war. I could relate to their pain, however, the books, articles and blogs clung to a more surface approach of addressing the desolation I was experiencing.

I attempted private counseling with my former premarital counselor, unsure if that was a good idea or not. Even those sessions did nothing but repeat what I had already read in the manual on misery and loss.

The ugliness of the despair that had become my daily existence made me feel like a pariah at times. It wasn't the fault of those around me. I turned down invitations to weddings, social outings and college homecoming celebrations, wearing my mask for those special occasions proved to be too much to bear. Ultimately, my pain pushed me into God's arms. I scoured the Bible for encouraging truths and instances of triumph to keep me going. I made the biblical character Ruth my new best friend. I would often re-read her story in the book of Ruth to remind myself that the death of one's spouse did not mean the end of God's promises for me nor the withdrawing of His provision. The following journal entry depicts my perusal of Isaiah 54:

> *February 22, 2009*
>
> *Jesus, in Isaiah 54, You promise to be my husband O Lord. You said that I will remember no more the reproach of my widowhood. You said You will call me back as if I was a wife deserted and distressed in spirit, a wife who married young, only to be rejected. You said that for a brief moment You abandoned me, but with deep compassion You will bring me back. You swore to not be angry with me, to never rebuke me again. You said that Your unfailing love will not be shaken, nor Your covenant of peace be removed. Lord Jesus, pray for me. I don't know what to say. Father, heal me. Show me how to live again. Father do that which You have promised. I trust You Lord. You will make a way.*
>
> *In Jesus' name,*
>
> *Amen*

The season after loss is one filled with unfamiliarity and painful rediscovery. When I lost my husband at the age of 24, I thought my world was over. In a way, **my** world was over. My way of doing everything was over. The life that I thought I was in control of was over. I resisted this reality. Everything was wrong! I couldn't see how this could possibly work out in my best interest. Job and Lamentations became my favorite books. Frankly, Job said things that I was too scared to say, so I figured I would just "pray the word back to Him" to avoid any issues with the Lord. Lamentations 3 created a vivid picture of how I could still trust and hope in the Lord against all odds. I read the Psalms and got a picture of David's passion-filled worship but also frequently saw it juxtaposed with gut-wrenching anguish. Zephaniah 3:17 told me that He was rejoicing over me with singing. What was there to sing about? I couldn't fathom why He would be so happy.

Then I looked at the calendar and realized that the days had continued to change and despite the greatest disruption in my life. I was still worshipping and clinging to Him. He was still on the throne. He was still God. He still caused the sun to rise daily and continued to synchronize my heartbeat to His own. I was *very* slowly learning to live and breathe again. A couple weeks passed, not without their own share of uncertainty and sorrow. Dealing with the various insurance investigations and public probing was tedious.

There were examinations at my job, graduate school, and even dentist's office to rule out that Brandon had not committed suicide that tragic night. I was also faced with turning *our* home into *my* home and continuing with graduate school while the storm raged around me. All of these agonizing moments tested every ounce of strength and faith I thought I had. There were instances in which a medical billing inquiry or an insurance document caused everything that happened that night to come flooding back. I would retreat back into my room. I would write in my journal, pray and cry until sheer emotional exhaustion would force me to sleep. I fought the urge to completely withdraw from society and allow my anguish to consume me daily.

At other times, cooking his favorite dish or hearing a love song would often make my heart just swell with the happiness that accompanied my marriage with him. I would think about the goodness he brought into my life and imagine how proud he would be to see that I had continued to live on. I tried to picture his face smiling at me in amazement at this new woman I was becoming. I prayed for a continuous strength that would give me a reason for the hope that I had. I trusted the adage that "what didn't kill me could only serve to make me stronger," so I kept moving on. Job said it best: *"though He slay me, yet will I trust Him."* I took that verse literally. Even though *He* had killed everything that had once defined me, I would continue to trust Him as he gave me new life. It was far from easy.

Those were the instances that were the hardest to keep my head up and my faith strong. I can't emphasize this enough. I eliminated bubble baths from my nighttime routine for a time because the temptation to allow the iridescent surface to permanently end my pain was too great. You will have many moments where you just want to quit. You may want to get off this crazy ride and say, "Enough! I don't want to play anymore!" Do not grow weary! The Lord, who created you and knows every path your life will take, will never abandon you. He promised *"all things work together for the good of them who love Him and are called according to His purpose."*[1] Hold Him to His promise.

Back at work, I saw the old looks of pity turning into new ones of awe and admiration. They didn't understand it, and neither did I. Despite fighting the tortuous process that losing Brandon had caused, somehow, I continued to live on. I still cried daily until I thought there was no way I could cry again. Fresh tears served me at breakfast, stopped by for lunch and then spent the night for old time's sake. (I discovered that if I cried during a hot shower, the ill effects of red, tear-rimmed eyes decreased drastically.) Yet and still, I knew that I wanted more than the sorrow and grief that I currently had. I determined to push myself beyond my limits and guess what? I was still here. I had finally made the Lord my life source. He became my life support. I was changing into a more confident, Christ-assured woman who had faced the lowest point of her life and had survived to talk about it. Night after night and tear after tear, He had been there. Each night, He met me in my closet as I sat on the floor and cried for lost opportunities and promises.

Despite the natural signs of growth and new life around me, I lamented over a life lost and the wreckage left behind. It was difficult to pay attention to the newness around me and still dwell in the darkness and death I felt. I quickly learned that I could not do both. I had to make a choice to live in the fresh life of the moment. I slowly but gradually began to put away our wedding pictures, scrapbooks of our courtship and any other memorabilia around our home. I could not continue to look back if I was to move on. What choice will you make? It was hard, but I was strengthened from my own pain. *Painful strength.*

The two words may seem like an oxymoron, but they mesh to push you beyond the limits, even the ones you've set yourself.

Do not try to make life predictable again; instead, flow with the new wind of change and trust your Maker to know exactly what He is doing. This is not to say that you should not deal with the anguish you may be feeling. On the contrary, let your tears water the ground for your next victory. Go on the journey. However, keep in mind your destination: the unique purpose you were created for, the unique solution you are destined to provide. Trust that God does not make mistakes. His way is perfect even if you cannot see it now. Seek Him in your pain. Challenge Him to be your Comforter as He stretches you into a new dimension and existence.

I wanted to live again, but I didn't know how exactly. You may be able to relate. I struggled to rediscover who I was now and who I was becoming. I had to look at every experience as brand new, even the ones that I had once shared with Brandon. I remember the first Sunday I drove to church alone. I wept the whole way there and almost didn't get out of the car.

February 22, 2009

Lord,

      I struggled so much to get to church today. I'm grateful for Your persistence and patience Holy Spirit. I realize that I have come to my end and now You begin. I want to dream again and trust You. I miss Brandon so much. It's hard to realize that he's been gone this long. I miss him and our dreams together. I have no other choice but to trust You and believe You. You know the thoughts and questions that race through my mind and heart daily. I want to hope for the future in You, it's just that I have no idea how that future looks like and what I should pray for. Can you show me Daddy? Lord, I don't want to get so deep in my grief that I don't allow room for Your grace that is sufficient for me. Am I burying my marriage Lord? Am I putting away all hopes of love, romance, children, companionship, and new beginnings? This season is definitely the lowest and most hurtful that I've experienced, but at the same time, it is the season that I can learn the most from being directly in Your presence. Help me to not rush through this process.

      Lord, hold me at night when I desire intimacy. I miss my husband's kisses, caresses, and everything else with him. As I see young families and as I watch my friends go on realizing some of the very hopes ad plans that Brandon and I desired to achieve, please remind me that You are not finished with me and that You already know the plans and promises You have for me. Help me to realize more than ever before that You are my source, strength, and shield. Help me to laugh again and find joy once more. Help me to learn how to be content with Your will. I love You with all that I am and not just what's left.

In Jesus' name,

Amen

Shopping for groceries and re-learning how to cook for one was a painful but necessary process. I could not continue to view myself as a wife but that did not mean that I had to leave behind the experiences that I lived and wisdom I gained. The process of rediscovering oneself can often mean merging the old with the new. **How can *you* rediscover yourself? What experiences will *you* draw upon to further bring clarity to who you are?**

Let's discover some concrete ways you can begin the process of rediscovery. Get a pen ready as I encourage you to participate with the questions posed. Use them as a way to shift your thinking and help you identify your personal lighthouse.

----

[1] Romans 8:28 NIV

Chapter 6:

Finding Your Lighthouse

Oftentimes, we have to change how we are looking at our circumstance in order to approach and experience it differently. Instead of asking yourself, *"Why me? Why now? Why this?"* think *"What is this affliction teaching me? What unique opportunity am I being trained for? What uncommon perspective and credibility is this situation bringing?"* Make your pain work for you. Force this hurtful moment to yield you something worthwhile in return.

The biblical book of Habakkuk encourages us to *"write the vision and make it plain on tablets, that he may run who reads it. For the vision is yet for an appointed time; but at the end it will speak, and it will not lie. Though it tarries, wait for it; because it will surely come, it will not tarry."*[1] I liken my vision to a lighthouse in the storm. Just like a lighthouse provides direction and piercing light in the darkest moments, identifying your vision helps you to navigate the dark depths of uncertainty and temporary loss of direction that accompanies a deep water experience.

Create a Vision Board

One strategy I adopted as I searched and waited for a new vision, was to create a vision board. I used a memo board to affix symbols that represented elements of importance to me. I used magazine clippings and images printed from online searches. I pinned dreams, aspirations and bucket-list items. In the middle of the board, I attached a prayer, which I used to pour out my insecurities, fears and questions. I asked God for His guidance in leading me and showing me what I should do next. I placed the board in a place of prominence and frequently visited it, especially during times when I felt completely lost or disheartened. My vision board served as a way to motivate me and guide me as I navigated the new waters I had been thrust into. It gave me a reason to keep moving.

I challenge you to create your own vision board. **What things continue to rise to the forefront of your mind as you envision your life past this temporary detour?** Your vision board can be as simple or elaborate as you desire. It is uniquely yours. Use it as a lighthouse to see past the troubled waters surrounding you. As you receive further revelation or clarity through your experience, you can make changes to it as you are led to. Often a change in the priority or arrangement of your personal value system may occur as things that you used to rank high on your list suddenly move to a lower tier as you evaluate the bigger picture. There may be things that seem totally impossible or out of reach. Include them anyway. Your vision is a guide; it is not a rigid list that must be read and executed with no outside help, imagination or passion. Do not become discouraged. If you see it, attach it to your board, and be open to taking the journey towards fully attaining it.

Tragic transitions violently push us on the path toward self-discovery. Tragedy removes the safety net that our previously uninterrupted lives made us take for granted. The painful season you're experiencing or that you have survived will further shape your unique contribution to this life. As I awkwardly settled into this chapter, introspection became an integral part of my existence. I asked questions and sought answers. As the raw wounds of pain very slowly began to ebb, I started to look at what had happened beyond the tangible facts of the accident. I became more aware of my life's purpose apart from my previous identity as Brandon's wife. I realized that I, too, had a unique aspiration and function. I was now open to learning exactly what it was.

Life is a series of experiences that won't make sense until you walk fully in your God-ordained destiny. What is it? What is your purpose? How do you figure out why you were placed on this earth? The answer is really simple: live. It sounds so trite but in actuality, many of us walk around in a corpse-like existence; always dreaming, wishing, and hoping but never actually *doing*. Live as if you were given every resource and gift you needed to walk in your destiny. Live as if fear weren't a factor. Live as if limitations didn't exist. The most important assignment you have in life is to live your life to the fullest potential.

Within you are contained dreams that can only be realized if you wake up and make them come true. Never discredit yourself. In spite of your background, failures or heartache, you can still achieve an intentional future if you choose. You have to combine that belief with your actions and your thoughts. I have realized that I really am my biggest critic. Even as I wrote these words, I battled myself: *"Will my story still be relevant? Am I expressing myself in a way that others can relate to and understand?"* I finally had to silence the voices of uncertainty and remind myself that my story had to be shared. This is not for personal glory or gain but out of obedience to the One who had trusted me with this trouble and was cheering me on to the finish line. Believing in oneself is only part of the trek. Think back on how many endeavors you talked yourself out of. **What stopped you from dreaming? What will it take for you to start over again?**

As I looked inwardly to ask myself the tough questions concerning my dreams and hopes, I struggled with the fact that I wasn't able to fulfill that dream as I lived in matrimonial happiness. *Why couldn't I stay married and still fulfill all of the plans God has for my life?* Honestly, I am still struggling with the answer to that question, and I have to make peace with the fact that I may never find the reason. What I do know is that I won't find out anything if I don't continue to put one foot in front of the other. It's not easy, I know. Honestly, there have been many moments in which I didn't keep swimming. Instead, I stopped to look back at events and memories that have already taken place. I lingered and lamented over the good times that were. As a result, I did not take advantage of creating new memories and new opportunities. It's like talking about how good last week's dinner was instead of making a new one with fresh ingredients. I tricked myself into thinking that today's appetite could be satiated by last week's meal.

I had to couple this change with faith and action. Even though it was easy for me to dream with no limits, the hard part was trusting in its manifestation without knowing how long it could take. Daily, you are given a brand new opportunity to approach the new day with a fresh perspective. **Are you maximizing this offer? If not, what is keeping you from taking the fullest advantage of each new day? What can you tangibly change about your routine in order to position yourself in taking these opportunities?** List them on the lines below.

_____

_____

_____

Wake Up!

Wake up believing you can't lose. Wake up to the newness this part of the journey brings. Until you wake up to the passions, quirks, and uniqueness within, who are you really? Push through the pain. I may not know your specific burden, but I do know that pain is essential for growth. I've experienced enough to learn that trouble and trying circumstances will come and go. However, if I allow myself to be defeated then who am I trusting in: God or my circumstance? Whenever you get down or you feel the familiar pull of doubt, worry, fear, anxiety or sadness; don't just yell at it. Fight it with action.

From the moment of his birth, the biblical Jacob lived life as if it owed him and not the other way around. He knew the destiny within him, and he was determined to stop at nothing until he saw it fully realized. Although not all of his choices can be celebrated, I often look at his biblical example and am encouraged to see that he overcame the odds of his birth order, circumstance, and even treachery to eventually wrestle with God Himself! Genesis 32 documents the detail of his nighttime encounter and paints a vivid picture of Jacob's sheer will and fight to live. He refused to let go until he was blessed. Despite the pain he surely faced and the uncertainty that probably plagued his mind in the midst of his struggle, he held on. Failure was not an option.

God never does the same thing twice. He loves showing off in your life and displaying His glory in your situations. He may not always give you what you want when you want it, but His nature is designed to meet your needs in a way that takes your breath away. I'm learning this for myself every day. This requires considerable patience and unequivocal trust, but it is so worth it. When you allow God to be God in your life, you allow the Master Potter to shape your life into what He has already seen it becoming. As you remain in His hand, the pounding, molding and beating of the clay can bring pain. The uncertainty of what you or your life will become invites fear, but ultimately surrendering to the fire of His refinement produces a masterpiece uniquely designed for His purpose and glory, allowing you to shine as a result.

Have you ever had a dream of something you wanted to accomplish or see? You worked at it, you hoped, you wished and you might have even prayed. Finally, after days, months or even years, your dream was realized. But a surprise was awaiting you. It was even better than you had imagined it!

This book was a dream of mine. I wrote a plan for it. I talked about it. I even referred to the success it would garner in bringing Christ fame as I shared how He displayed His glory in my life. Yet, if I had never typed a word on my laptop, it would have still been a dream. The process wasn't easy by any means, but each time I felt like "taking a break,"; I envisioned myself holding the finished copy of my book... no, His book. I would think of every night I cried and every prayer I prayed; and then I simply had to push myself. I wanted to give up so often. I even tried running away from the whole thing; but like the biblical Jonah, I was inclined to keep my vow to the Lord and finally be obedient to His will and His way. I took very long breaks between and stopped many times. Even during the long breaks, which sometimes lasted weeks or months, God was faithful in His pursuit of my obedience and trust.

I got encouragement from friends who reminded me of my purpose and the need to share my story. I asked the Lord for a community of friends who would encourage me to stay focused and keep pushing past the pain of my present circumstances to keep my eyes on the prize. *"I'm not saying that I have this all together, that I have it made. But I am well on my way, reaching out for Christ, who has so wondrously reached out for me. Friends, don't get me wrong: By no means do I count myself an expert in all of this, but I've got my eye on the goal, where God is beckoning us onward— to Jesus. I'm off and running, and I'm not turning back."[2]*

Can you imagine what life would be like if you did even 25% of the things you always dreamed of doing? What impact would be made on the world, as we know it? Use the lines below to take a moment to make a list of your dreams and passions. (You may need more room. Feel free to continue your list on a separate sheet of paper.) After creating your list, give each goal a category title. This will help you to further hone in on that unique area that drives you and will aid you in attaining an even clearer direction towards realizing your dreams.

What drives me? What is my "one thing?" What am I passionate about? How can my painful season push me towards attaining the dreams and visions within me?

_____

_____

_____

As you make this list, be sure to look for any overarching themes. What do these categories tell you about yourself?

_____

_____

_____

It doesn't matter how big, how small, how likely or seemingly impossible it may be. He would have known that He could be the only one to help you to accomplish it. So, don't fear. Don't shut the door to possibilities before you even open it. Trust Him to be faithful. Surround yourself with positive people and environments. You have to win! You cannot give up. If you do, who will do what only you can? Lean on Him, but press on. Write it down and ask the Lord for wisdom as you prepare a plan inspired by Him to attain it.

_____

_____

_____

What's so special about you?

There are unique gifts and talents embedded in you. What are they? They may seem weird or different to others, but there is a purpose in why God has given you a special talent. Your mission is to pool your resources, apply your talents and watch God honor your faith by blowing your mind. How many of these on your list are not yet receiving the fullest attention. How has this affected you? **What do you plan to do in order to change?**

_____

_____

_____

You have to take time to reevaluate who you are and what is important to you. It is so easy to play it safe, to never try something new. Routines, although comforting and safe, can be the catalysts of a battle you will lose if you do not change your thinking and approach. Change your route. We are often so used to being in autopilot that we don't even notice the details of our journey. I would often change the way I drove home so as not to have to pass by the accident site. I did this both to preserve my mind and heart. I learned how to change my routines and strategies while all the while, keeping my focus on my purpose. Try new things as you experience this new journey. I began to rediscover Atlanta and visit places and attend events that I never felt inclined to do before. I made new friends while cherishing the old. I traveled and tried to expand my culinary palette. I changed my hair and redecorated my home. I had to have a tangible demonstration of the changes happening behind the scenes of my life.

I am humbled when I think of the choices I could have made after losing Brandon. I am proud to see the ones that I did make and excited about the ones I have yet to make. That is not to say that life was perfect and I never made a single mistake, on the contrary, mistakes became frequent learning opportunities that took off the mask I had gotten accustomed to wearing. I learned who Nathalie was. I was honest with myself and others. I stepped out of my comfort zone. **What choices have your deep water experience caused you to make? How have those choices helped to shape your view on your current circumstance? List them on the lines below.**

_____

_____

_____

Often, I wonder what other paths my life could have taken, and then it hits me- I am still living! My life is not over. Things that could have taken me out, but they didn't. Who am I to not have the tenacity to exhaust every moment as a chance to be fully stretched and pulled into my destiny? Of course, this is easier said than done. It takes work. It takes waking up with a plan to work the vision and not just dream about it.

----

[1] Habakkuk 2: 2,3 NIV

[2] Philippians 3:13,14 The Message Bible

Chapter 7:

Swimming Lessons

A fter identifying the vision I needed to strive towards completing, I searched for ways to realize them. I read books. I spoke to trusted friends and advisors and increased my quiet time with the Lord. I collected these lessons and frequently revisited them as I was faced with new challenges and decisions. Ultimately, I had to learn to swim in the new waters I found myself in.

Chronicle your journey. The journals I kept after Brandon's death served both as therapy and a testimony to how far I had made it. Each time it got to a place where I said, *"God I can't take another step,"* I would read an entry in my own handwriting that spoke victory over something that I never thought I could conquer. Document the day, and record your most raw feelings. When you succeed, look back at the place that was the tailgate site of your victory. If journal writing doesn't appeal to you, use your own creativity to accomplish the same task. Blogging, vlogging, poetry, songwriting, painting, drawing and dancing are just some examples of how you can capture the crude essence of your experience in order to gain strength or inspiration from it at a later time.

Set a marker to symbolize your transition. After Jacob's nighttime encounter with God, he built an altar and renamed the place, *Peniel*, which means "face of God." He said: "*For I have seen God face to face, and my life is preserved.*" [1] His wrestling match with God forever changed his life, and he built a monument to stand as witness to the fact that something out of the ordinary had occurred there. As I wrestled with God, I knew He would win every match; but there still existed a deep need to get all of my feelings and frustrations out.

March 15, 2009

Lord Jesus,

I am really, really missing Brandon right now. I miss everything about him. This new season I'm in is raw with pain, loneliness, frustration, tears, and sorrow. When I think of anything that has to do with him, I just want to cry, and I do. This bed that I am laying in is so empty without him. I don't want to fantasize about my life with someone else, someone else's children, a different home, yet I battle with hope, and still believing in a brighter tomorrow in You Lord. My body misses his touch, my heart his kindness, and this house lacks his presence. Father, hold me tonight. I'm in a place I never thought I'd be. It's hard for me to come to grips with the fact that <u>my</u> husband is gone! I know he was Yours first Lord, but he loved me so much and I loved him. Show me a vision of hope through this pain Lord. Hide me under the shadow of Your wings; never let me go...

I can vividly recall the day I chose to remove the golden bands of commitment that I had lovingly donned on my wedding day. It was the weekend after the funeral. Friends and family had all left to return to their lives; I was finally home alone. I remember sitting on my couch, looking down at my hands and noticing the sparkle that soon blurred as I wept. I knew that if I were to move from this place, I had to lay to rest this marker of another place in my life journey. The resistance I felt as I pulled first one band, and then another, mirrored the feelings in my own heart at the seemingly final sentence to my marriage and happiness. The suntanned bands left behind echoed the memories of love and innocence that I had experienced. Even as those eventually faded, I knew that I needed to set up a new marker, a new indication of the hope that I now daily relied on.

I purchased a pearl ring to encourage me as I submitted to the process of change and restoration. This ring would symbolize the patience I would have to exhibit under the pressure I was feeling in the most tumultuous storm I had ever experienced. It represented a fresh, new life formed in the secret places deep in the darkness of the ocean. Yet, despite the darkness of the ocean lairs in which it was formed, it yielded a treasure that would be ready in time. *"I will give you hidden treasures, riches stored in secret places, so that you may know that I am the LORD, the God of Israel, who summons you by name."[2]* **What will you use as a symbol of your transitioning journey? It can represent where you are or where you are going.**

When I look down at my ring, I feel a mixture of feelings. When I feel immensely discouraged, I try to remind myself of its purpose and promise. Other times, I honestly get frustrated because it is easy to remember what used to be in its place. However, whatever my mood is, my symbol of transition continues to serve as a tangible reminder of my refusal to stop hoping for joy. It also displays my unrelenting determination to keep living a full life.

Praise and worship. What do you do when you feel you've prayed every prayer and poured out your heart before the King of Kings? You worship. In all transparency, I admit that there are moments when it is a struggle to open my mouth and say: "I love You. I thank You. I trust You." In light of the turmoil that surrounds me, it takes everything I have. However, my sacrifice of praise is always welcomed by His holy presence. When I declare my love for Him through song, quiet meditation or in a loud voice of adulation, I change the atmosphere of my circumstance. I declare, as it says in Romans 4:17, "...those things that do not exist as though they did." In my case this is joy, thanksgiving and peace. My pastor always says, "It is impossible to praise God and be depressed at the same time." I have found this to be true every time.

It just seems that the Lord is such a part of me now that even when I want to be mad at Him, I can't. On the contrary, I cling to Him stubbornly, like my very life depends on Him. It does. I throw before Him and wash His feet with my prayers like the woman with the alabaster box. I scream out in pain like a woman in childbirth who must fight through the pain to bring forth the new life in her. No matter how much it kills me, my soul cries out His name. Job says "...*indeed this will turn out for my deliverance.*" [3] What is this phenomenon? Why don't I just "curse God and die" or succumb to my circumstance like Job's wife encouraged him to do in the midst of the stormiest season of his life? No, instead, I worship Him. After countless shouting matches, I lay my head on His lap full of grace and mercy, and I weep. He is always ready to comfort and direct me once again. I speak to Him from my heart. I sing. I pray. I sleep. I dream. I let Him into the part of me that only He has a key to.

My pain is real; my God is bigger. I have to trust Him. Somehow, everything I have experienced is a part of His master plan. I remember being frustrated as I tried to find my redefinition in Him. God has such a unique way of truly working out all things for our good. No matter how painful or unpleasant a situation may seem to be playing out, remember it is all in your perspective. This is not to say that every scenario will make you see the colorful rainbows and cuddly puppies. Gradually, you will see it His way. He will grant you a new view that will take you to a new level in your faith.

Plan for pain. Having a plan does not mean that you should live in constant expectation of pain and turmoil, but you should be aware of your triggers and immerse yourself so deep in the Word that you have a ready response to the thoughts of fear and worry. At my most vulnerable times, it wasn't usually the best time to re-watch my wedding day DVD or to reread love letters from Brandon. I knew that engaging in those activities at my weakest moments essentially activated hours and/or days of grief and anguish. I knew the importance of dealing with my pain, but *purposely* pushing myself into a place of turmoil was typically not the best way to allow the process of healing to naturally occur.

Instead, when I would feel the familiar pangs of fear, pain, and sadness threatening to rain down on me; I would immediately reach for my journal and Bible. I would also call a trusted friend, pray until I felt peace, get out of the house or a combination of all of those. I knew that if I lingered in my grief, it would be relatively easy to convince myself that my life was over and that that the sun would never shine again. **What do you usually do? Are those habits positive or negative? What else can you do as you plan for the pain that follows uncomfortable and unwelcome transition?**

Take a history class. No, you don't have to add another commitment to your already full load! What I mean is that you need to take a look back at the Lord's presence in your life. Look back at all of the instances He's provided you with direct comfort and guidance. This is the hardest tool to learn to how to use, because in the midst of turmoil, what could be harder than reminding yourself of all the times He had never let you down? Mastery of this tool will take time, however, it will eventually be the most useful. It will remove all possible invasions of doubt and second-guessing because God's word will prove itself in your life.

I meditated on Isaiah 50:2: "Do I lack the strength to rescue you?" I viewed that statement as a direct question being asked of me by the most High. Each time I felt like I was drowning, I would ask myself: "Does He lack the strength to rescue you?" With a resounding "no", I would push forward another day. He had never failed me. Why should I ever give in to the defeat which doubt wanted me to embrace? Now, this is not to say that I never stopped moving. Of course I did. I wept. I questioned. I was angry. What I am saying is that you are now reading this book because I didn't stop. As I mentioned earlier, I paused many, many times; but I kept going. I want to encourage you to keep going. It may not seem as if you have a reason to live. Losing your child, your spouse, your parent or sibling rocks the sea of tranquility that you were resting on. Not getting the job, getting a negative doctor's report and having your heart broken by someone you love are moments that do not add to your peace.

Even when you don't understand, trust Him. From my own experience, I know this concept is tremendously hard. There were times in this season of my life that I fought with God and His sovereignty. In all honesty, at times, I still do. Daily, I have to fight my innate desire to take control. I have to let Him lead and steer completely. After all, He knows the destination! His way of doing things, which typically does not involve a clear roadmap complete with rest stops and landmarks, is not always the easiest choice. Even still, I trust Him.

Sleep. Don't underestimate the importance of sleep as you experience the rough waters of your storm. Jesus Himself slept through a storm that His disciples, and fellow boat passengers were quite literally freaking out about. He modeled the essence of stubbornly holding onto peace despite the turmoil that surrounded Him. How was He able to do that? Matthew 8:23-27 in the Amplified Bible lays out the story like this:

And after He got into the boat, His disciples followed Him.

24 And suddenly, behold, there arose a violent storm on the sea, so that the boat was being covered up by the waves; but He was sleeping.

25 And they went and awakened Him, saying, Lord, rescue and preserve us! We are perishing!

26 And He said to them, Why are you timid and afraid, O you of little faith? Then He got up and rebuked the winds and the sea, and there was a great and wonderful calm (a perfect peaceableness).

27 And the men were stunned with bewildered wonder and marveled, saying, What kind of Man is this, that even the winds and the sea obey Him!

I can imagine what being on that boat must have felt like. What the disciples thought would be a simple journey across the bay, suddenly and violently morphed into a deadly encounter that seemingly no one was prepared for! The dark clouds and whirling winds of the storm tossed their boat about like a leaf in the river. The back and forth motion that had once been comforting, even expected, now roughly shook every sense of stability they had once confidently felt. Their eyes darted from the raging, blackened skies above to the tempest churning all around them. Waves as tall as hills and maybe even mountains plummeted upon them. Surely this was the end. I picture the dialogue amongst His followers to have gone something like this:

This is it! We're going to die!
Wait! We are not alone! We have Jesus, remember? He's on the boat with us.
He who heals the sick, raises the dead, and walks in the supernatural can save us; isn't that the message we've been sharing?
Isn't that why we gave up our plans, our former lives, our everything for?
Wait, where is He?
Can you find Him in this storm? It's so dark!

He should be right over...

I think I see Him...impossible! What?!

Is He sleeping?!

Doesn't He see what's happening all around us? How could He?

Doesn't He care?

Don't our lives, service and sacrifice mean anything to Him?

How can He sleep during a time like this?

Wake Him up!

Jesus! Jesus! Help us! We're going to die if You don't do something now!

In instances such as this, the disciples needed Him to see that they were the victims, and that He should be doing His best to make an already painful interruption less inconvenient. Can you relate? Can't He see that you've suffered enough?

No matter what, remember who controls the storm. Whose voice do the wind and seas obey? Observe the reactions to the storm that the disciples express. Look familiar? Now, look at the Master. What behaviors does He exhibit? **What is this telling us about what should happen when we face storms in life?**

He is God, and He is in control. His thoughts really are higher than ours. He is merciful in His love towards us. He goes before us and prepares us. He already knows the assignments, responsibilities, changes and challenges you will have to endure. He is not surprised or caught off guard by anything even if you are. Choose to rest and trust in Him despite what you may see with your eyes. Let your life belong completely to Him, no matter what storms threaten to tear down your shelter. When you do this you are serving as a testimony to others of strength, courage, vulnerability and true faith.

Smell the flowers. In the aftermath of a season that promised to yield only death and sorrow, it was essential to involve new life and new reasons to hope again. I adopted a new puppy to bring joy, laughter and playful mischief back into my life. I started buying fresh flowers to fill the rooms of my home with God-inspired canvases of color and creativity. I filled my home with music that created an atmosphere of peace. I covered my walls (tastefully) with framed scriptures to encourage and remind me of the Father's promises to me. I did everything I could think of to replicate the symptoms of the natural season I currently found myself in. Spring entered my home, sweeping away the coldness that winter had left behind. Like the fresh, lingering smell rain leaves behind after a storm, my life began to truly follow the footsteps of a God who had intricately involved Himself in every aspect of my existence to bring me to the horizon of true joy again.

The editing and revising of each chapter of your life can often allow some uncomfortable primping and pruning. In the end, it will be worth it. Finish the book. Read the last chapter. Don't cheat yourself of an ending worthy of such a unique beginning. Keep living. Do the things that will put the sparkle back into your eyes. These things can be as refreshing as a spa appointment or as fulfilling as a grande mocha soy latte no whip, extra mocha, a taste of caramel and a sprinkling of chocolate shavings! (My personal favorite☺) Command each day and assign each hour to bring you into the fullness of joy and fulfillment that you can experience. Edit the empty spots of your life and cause them to be filled with the things that matter, which includes quiet time. **What matters to you? What can you include/ introduce into your routine that will usher in new life?** Use them as tools to encourage and propel you on your journey.

Manage your time. Use time as a tool given to maximize each moment you're given. Set clear and tangible goals for yourself daily and weekly. I struggle with this concept just as much if not more than the average person. I have noticed several patterns when I do manage my time and when I don't. I feel more accomplished, and I am astonished to see the things I am able to get done when I write it down and set a date for its completion. The entire process adds value to my life and encourages me to want to create similar occurrences to replicate lasting results of happiness, pride, and goal achievement.

Of course, the opposite is in effect for the moments in which time manages me. I look up at a clock and get angry at how fast the hands are moving. I tend to blame every available outside factor for my own personal failures. The weather, PMS, traffic and even my dog become culpable agents to the delay I incur. Instead of exultant feelings, I am plagued with frustration, anxiety and even doubt in my own capabilities. One way I try to counter these behaviors is through accountability partners. I have a select group of friends who I have chosen to share my goals. They check in on me during the day or week to help me assess my progress and to encourage me in moments I haven't accomplished as much as I wanted to. Honestly, I don't always look forward to their calls or text messages; but I do realize the necessity of accountability. Surround yourself with "future friends," those individuals who are walking with you and propelling you into your tomorrow. These friends should not be afraid to tell you the truth, aptly seasoned with love and tact.

Make a list below of at least 5 individuals in your life who are helping you walk into your tomorrow.

1._____

2._____

3._____

4._____

5._____

Share your story. You may be thinking, "That's the last thing I want to do." In actuality, what you will pleasantly discover is that as you share the overarching theme of your painful interruption, it gradually won't hurt as much. You will realize that God has enabled you to become stronger than you ever thought possible. Take your time and share only the parts of the your story you feel led to tell. There is no set formula on how to convey your experience or designated platform on how to relay it. You may want to write a letter to a friend going through a rough time, participate on a panel addressed to a similar audience, casually talk to your neighbor, host a get-together with your close friends or start a blog. No matter how you chose to express yourself, do it. You have to do what you were born to do, if you don't it won't be done. Your deep-water experience is essential to this world. Approach every waking moment as a divine opportunity to serve others from the unique vantage point of reference your circumstance gave you.

You will learn the most essential lesson on this journey: *your pain had nothing to do with you.* Your pain, just like Christ's pain at the cross, was to draw others to the Father. You will walk taller and hold your head up higher even when you may be experiencing pain that would debilitate others. You will become a living, breathing example of Christ's strength and will directly serve as an example of a life submitted to Him. Wow...who would have thought? As you share your story to those who you feel led to, you will watch the reactions of awe and utter respect as they look to you, and then past you, for a glimpse of the foundation you stand on.

You'll shake your head and wonder what they see. They'll tell you that they could never have done it if it happened to them. You'll remember the tears you cried just last night. You might even try to remind them of how low you were. From my own personal experience, they won't see it. They'll see how high the Father has elevated you, and they will want to know how He did it. Unknowingly, you've just shared your faith. You have encouraged someone who you wouldn't normally talk to. You just gave someone a lifeline you didn't know they needed. Let the Lord lead you as He showcases His glory in your life. **How do you want to share your story with others?** If you're not quite ready, continue to document your experience so that, when you are ready, you will have a reference point created in real-time.

Next, things are about to get warmer as we turn up the heat on certain aspects of my journey that exposed me to the elements. I was finally stripped of the remnants of the cosmetic shell I had encased around my life. I had to go through this stage in order to get to the core of my pain and learn the lessons it was teaching about me about myself, my faith, and my God.

Here we go.

----

[1] (Reference Genesis 32:30)

[2] Isaiah 45:3 NIV

[3] Job 13:15, 16 NIV

Chapter 8:

An Anchor in the Storm

The next leg of my journey gave me the most time to relax and reflect, or so I thought... The lazy pace of these days forced me to get real and revisit themes that I had previously skimmed over due to time constraints or misaligned priorities. Now, it was time to get focused. I analyzed patterns of behavior and my subsequent reactions in order to identify areas where growth was needed, and things that needed to change completely. I frequently looked back at where I was a year or two ago mainly to assess my state of mind and to contrast it with where I currently was. Recently, looking back over some of the journals I kept before getting married revealed a startling truth: *I was not as ready as I sometimes think I was.*

It can be amazing and sobering how reflecting on your past can reveal things that you did not notice about yourself before. I can see now that I was still growing in my level of intimacy with my Savior, and that presently I am much closer than I ever was. Needless to say, when I was in the experience of the season, I just knew that I was on track to be "wife of the year". I mean, I was able to check off my Christianity, virtue, and submitted lifestyle to both Christ and my husband. I was the perfect candidate, right? Not exactly. See, my priorities were out of line.

As I dug deeper to the heart of the matter, I observed the sparse prayer journal entries and the long intervals in between devotions. I was so caught up in being the model wife and helpmate that I had put my primary relationship with God on the back burner. I relied on my husband's faith and prayers more than my own. I remember feeling so safe in my existence. I was consumed with having everything in place to create the perfect picture. I wanted an even number of children because I hate odd numbers. I wanted a family dog to resemble the ones found in the commercials. I eventually desired a white picket fence be installed to keep our cute yard intact.

Regrettably, I had pushed God out of my marriage and relegated Him to the background. Sure, He was there on my Sunday morning church outings and the occasional crisis call. Yet, His place as the King of my heart had been replaced by my own doing. I still called on Him and brought

Him up to speed on the happenings of my life, but I didn't consistently pursue a true, covenant relationship with Him as I watched my own husband do. Instead, to my dismay, I had chosen to make my husband and my dream of our future family, my all. I had forsaken all others as wives and husbands are called to do; yet, sadly, I had added God to the list of exclusion. I was out of order and now had a chance to set things right again with my First Love...but how?

Psalm 51 was a good start; I've included an excerpt from
The Message Bible:
Generous in love—God, give grace!
Huge in mercy—wipe out my bad record.
Scrub away my guilt,
soak out my sins in your laundry.
I know how bad I've been;
my sins are staring me down.
[4-6] *You're the One I've violated, and you've seen*
it all, seen the full extent of my evil.
You have all the facts before you;
whatever you decide about me is fair.
I've been out of step with you for a long time,
in the wrong since before I was born.
What you're after is truth from the inside out.

Enter me, then; conceive a new, true life.
God, make a fresh start in me,
shape a Genesis week from the chaos of my life.
Don't throw me out with the trash,
or fail to breathe holiness in me.
Bring me back from gray exile,
put a fresh wind in my sails!
Going through the motions doesn't please you,
a flawless performance is nothing to you.
I learned God-worship
when my pride was shattered.
Heart-shattered lives ready for love
don't for a moment escape God's notice.

My personal tragedy led me to this place of restoration. I pray that yours does the same for you. I began by renewing my marriage vows to Christ. Everything would be new this time. I invited Him to once again become "*the One whom my soul loves[1],*" not because of my loss but rather, in spite of it. I prayed a simple prayer welcoming Him back into the fullness of my heart and seeking forgiveness for the moments I had fallen back. I believed that He heard and answered my prayers as soon as I uttered them. The prayer was the easiest part of this undertaking. The hard part would be walking it out. I acknowledged His sovereignty and wisdom far beyond my own. I reflected on His promises to complete what He started in my life. I thought of His mercy, when I was clearly in the wrong. I saw images of His grace, as His faithfulness towards me was revealed daily. I remembered how He walked with me through unknown valleys of sadness and over mountains of loneliness. I listened as He gently, patiently showed me how to love Him back. Friend, this took time. It was, by no means, an overnight process. There were many false starts, but I was determined. I had to learn to trust the One who had broken my heart, shattered my dreams and invited chaos and turmoil into my life. How is that even possible? Could I let Him in once more? What if He did it again?

You may be nodding your head in agreement as you recognize questions that you've asked yourself as you traverse your own oceans of sickness and loss. I want to encourage you. You're not crazy! Yes I know what others around you may be saying. Your thoughts are anything but positive these days. However, remember that God is still at work in your life. His intention is not to hurt you but to propel you into your destiny. Pain is a disagreeable, yet necessary byproduct. In this case, your journey is just as important as your destination. Forgiveness of self and others is a cornerstone in the rebuilding process.

I invite you to join me in my renewal of faith. Reprioritize your value system, and make adjustments where necessary. Although you may not have strayed from God as I did, you may have shut out family or friends who tried to walk with you in your journey. You may have said or done some things you now wish you could take back. Don't be held up by your past errors and shortcomings. Seek forgiveness from those you may have offended, and if they are no longer around or reachable; forgive yourself. Allow yourself to begin anew. The freedom you will feel will be incomparable as you allow true healing to take place in the broken areas of your heart.

Please be advised, however, this is not a one time deal. I cannot emphasize this enough! Daily, I have to make the choice to seek God first and to keep our relationship fresh and first in my life. You must do the same. I believe the only way to hear His voice is to be close enough to feel His heartbeat. As you make mistakes along the way, repent for your sin. Renew your heart and mind in Christ, and begin again. Don't become captive to your faults. **On the following lines below, make a list of those you need to seek forgiveness from and/or the things you need to forgive yourself for. What personal action steps can you commit to taking in order to enjoy true freedom?**

_____

_____

_____

As I became liberated from my unfaithfulness, I was reacquainted with my original identity as a child of God before becoming a wife and widow. I examined what my life meant now and how my new dreams and visions fit in. This moment of submersion presented me with the task of achieving that delicate balance between new adventures and my priorities as a Christian and servant. Life was beginning to mean so much more to me because I could finally see that it had never been about me, my personal comforts, wants or desires. Instead, it had always been about fully committing to a God who wanted my absolute love and conviction above all.

It dawned on me that life would never be the same again. I mean, of course, I realized that fact on the tragic January evening. Yet, it seemed like now more than ever, it had truly begun to settle in my mind. I had to begin living in the perspective and purpose God had given me. I needed to put the new knowledge that these life lessons were teaching me to work. I could no longer just sit back and be a spectator. I had to take responsibility for my personal faith walk and attend to the neglected areas. I resisted this change and cried many tears of sadness, frustration and doubt. I just wanted everything to be better fast. I knew that Brandon wasn't coming back, but I still struggled with what life would now mean without him. I resisted the new place I now found myself in. I never asked for this. None of this was in my plan.

God had broken me in more ways than one, and now He was slowly rebuilding me to become the woman after His own heart, just as He always intended. I was re-learning how to seek Him first in every way and allow Him to meet all of my needs. This was by no means a straightforward undertaking. I still wanted Him to just snap His fingers and make me who He wanted overnight. I wanted to automatically pray everyday, share my faith, laugh at trouble, and trust Him easily with no effort of my own. Thankfully, my request was not met.

July 30, 2014

Father, thank You for waking me up this morning and taking me step by step down the path You have decided for me. Lord, I repent for my fear, my frustration, and almost giving up. I'm sorry for not being thankful for every part of this process. I repent for not seeing Your BIG picture. I submit anew to Your will. I thank You for showing me that You see farther than me. Thank You for keeping me under Your shadow, even when I resisted Your peace. I will rest in You. I will abide in You. You are in control. God, You are doing it and I will see and know it. Grant me Your perspective. Show me what You see about me. I ask for Your forgiveness for speaking things I knew nothing about in my frustration and anxiety. Lord, today, I renew my mind in You. Write Your word over my heart so that I may hear clearly from You. I trust in You and I will not be moved or shaken come what may. Thank You for Your daily bread. Thank You for Your divine protection.

In Jesus' name I pray,

Amen and Amen

God was showing me that His thoughts truly were better and higher than mine. I had to trust that He had thought of everything. He could have very easily prevented the tragedy that took away my status as wife. However, He chose not to.

He could just speak and everything would be made right in my life; yet He didn't. I started to look at the big picture my life presented, and I discovered that maybe there was more to what I was seeing. I began to see that God had put into place certain key events in my life in order to bring me into the fullness of His dream for me. But, first I would need to give up everything once more.

----

[1] Song of Solomon 3:4, NKJV

Emerging

Emerge
verb \[ih-murj]

1: to rise or come forth from or
as if from water or other liquid

2: to come up or arise

3: to rise, as from an inferior
or unfortunate state or condition

Chapter 9:

Treading Water

G od was writing my life story, and although I absolutely abhorred the current chapter; I would have to trust that He knew what was best. I was slowly realizing that I was never in charge. This storm was changing the direction of my life and plans especially in the area of relationships. While I was beginning to see the positive signs of change with my First Love, I saw nothing but a foggy haze surrounding anyone else. After 2 ½ years of brokenness, confusion, loneliness and exclusion; I wanted to once again feel that I was loved and desired by a man. I battled these new feelings, because as my personal relationship with Christ flourished, I still felt as if something tangible was missing. Naturally, I thought it was a man.

I didn't really seek God in this department. Of course, I asked Him what was taking so long and to give me a sign that revealed who my next husband was to be. He only gave me Himself. You see, I thought that I had learned my lesson and now should be rewarded with a second chance at love and marriage. I promised that I would not make the same mistakes again. I would keep Him first and my husband second. I had now entered a new portion of the journey that was putting to the test everything I had previously rejoiced about in my newly committed walk with Christ. I was being challenged to trust His will and timing in my heart This time, it was with the knowledge of my past failures and pain. I had to give Him the secret part of my heart, the part that had been exposed for such a brief moment in time but was returned broken beyond recognition. Friend, I wish I could tell you that I passed that test with flying colors; but I did not. I continued to separate my devotion to God with my heart of flesh. There was still a tiny part of me that did not trust Him to fix *everything* concerning true love and romance. The ricochet of the attack on my heart had penetrated deeper than even I could realize at the time. While I allowed God into the entryway of my heart's home, He was still not permitted to have a seat.

I was trying to do things my way in this one area of my life. I submitted everything else to God, but my heart and future love belonged to me. Unknowingly, I was trying to fill a void only the One who created it could fill. In came the lonely nights of desiring intimacy and closeness with a

man who would keep me safe and hold me tight. I thought
a new relationship would help me to move further along
the road to recovery. My first attempt at this proved to be
complicated as soon as I made it clear which lines would
not be crossed. I battled living a life of purity after having
been introduced to the joys of the marriage bed. Although
my marriage had ended, my physical desires had not. I
couldn't forget what I knew, but I also chose not to share or
experience passion with a man who was not my husband.
Needless to say, that relationship ended quickly. As the
years passed, I went on a few more dates; but something
was still missing.

I moved from job to job. I joined clubs and cultural
organizations. I tried to relocate several times. I attempted
online dating (nothing wrong with it, just not for me). I
visited the Singles Ministry at my church. Try as I might,
nothing stopped the pain. I couldn't understand it. After all,
I was trying to keep living and get back to life as normal.
What was wrong?

Gradually, I noticed the patterns behind my pain.
I saw how my distrust of God in this major area of my
life was wreaking havoc everywhere else. Ultimately, my

frustrations drove me back to my Father. I finally submitted the secret part of my heart to Him and allowed Him to show me how to balance my desires with His timing. I started to do things His way. I slowly began to re-enter the social scene. It was awkward and guilt-ridden at first. I wasn't sure if I should be going out, and I detested being single at events that I had once entered on the arm of my late husband. The etiquette and propriety on "dealing with a widow" often clouded others' attempts at friendship and openness with me. Eventually, I released everyone else's definition of what was proper and timely and started to step out in confidence that everything would be okay. I listened when He instructed me to rest. There were periods where I didn't have a traditional work schedule and title; but thanks to those moments, this book was made possible. I didn't understand His ways, but I came to respect His authority over my life.

I have come to the place where I may not particularly enjoy where I am, but I am determined to let God strengthen me, help me and uphold me. He promises that no matter what comes, He is there. Any attempt to fill a void with anything other than Him is done in vain. This is a constant journey; you must keep moving. He's right there, ever near, cheering you on and reminding you of the destiny you shared together before you were born.

He's not just there to stand by and watch you in your anguish and pain. Although if you're honest with yourself, it may seem like that at times. There are still times loneliness sets in so heavily that I forget what it was like to be held by someone, to walk with someone designed just for me. I haven't been on a real date in years...*years*! With each passing birthday, I wonder "When will it happen for me again?" Is there something I need to do to further this process along? I'm quickly reminded that there is no substitute for God's perfect will and presence in my life. I let it go. He has to be enough. He has to be my all. While I do want to love again, I know that my future husband can never take God's place in my life.

June 2, 2009

Father,

I thank You for Your grace and Your infinite patience. Lord, You are walking me through this season and taking me by the hand. Lord as I grapple with my feelings and the difficulties of everything, fill my love tank to overflowing. Meet every one of my needs. Cover me and grant me fulfilling relationships that are sent by You. Relationships that usher in my destiny and the next phases of my life directly orchestrated by You. I trust You. I need to learn to wait graciously and patiently. Fill my heart with peace and give me a spirit of acceptance that I might know happiness even when things don't happen fast enough to suit me. Show me how to be proactive in my waiting. I know that this season isn't something that I should bypass or rush through. I wait on You and Your timing. Help me to enjoy these moments you have me in.

In Jesus' name,

Amen

As you can read in my entry, I still believe that relationships are from God. The difference is that, now, I am not viewing them as the solution to my pain or an escape from the path God currently has me on. Relationships with others are necessary for growth and community. As you navigate through these waters, continue to be open to the new people you will encounter. However, use wisdom in choosing whom you invite to join you. I proceeded very cautiously. I have had to learn everything all over again. How can I tell if a guy likes me? What are his intentions? What is his purpose in my life? Is my heart right? Am I ready? How do I love again? What if I never marry again? These are questions that I still often wrestle with.

I may never know the answer to these questions, but I do realize that I cannot live my life on pause waiting to pick up from the last happy scene. Life still goes on. I don't know what comes next, but then again, did I ever? What have you been using to try to fill the void of your personal disruption? Memories of the past? Career? Relationships? Longings of a future that can no longer occur quite like you imagined? Whatever it is, you have to understand that there is nothing that can undo what already happened. However, there is Someone who can undo the pain it caused and walk with You to the next stop on your trek.

Pray this prayer with me:

Heavenly Father, I need You in a major way. I am still hurting. I have tried to dull the pain by filling in the space that belongs to You with _____. I can see now that there is no substitute for Your love and presence in my life. I submit my life to You and ask that You become King of my heart in every way. I hold nothing back. I invite You to reside in the deepest, most secret part of me, the part no one else knows about. I don't know where to go from here, but You do. Holy Spirit, teach me to trust You more; show me how to pray daily, read Your word and have a stronger, closer relationship with You. I understand that this is a process, but I believe that You can heal me completely. I submit to Your way. Show me the things, people, and thoughts that I need to let go of. Introduce me to Your perspective on my life. Show me what You see about me and my circumstance. May Your perfect will be done in Your perfect timing in my life. You know the things that I still want, but I trust that You know best. I am Your vessel; fill me to overflowing with Your comfort, love, joy, and contentment. Teach me how to be at peace whether things abase or abound. Most of all, I love You and thank You for hearing my prayer and pursuing me patiently and persistently. I pray all of this in Jesus' name, Amen.

Chapter 10:

A New Destination

I can close my eyes and remember it like it yesterday. Overwhelming feelings of sadness, longing, loneliness and a strange feeling of missing out on something began to settle in. Still photo-moments of my past bombarded my mind as I struggled to embrace my new existence and future. Now that my head was above the surface again, I realized that I could not remain where I was. I fight the tendency to want to look back and stay there. I realize that I can't go back. I'm not the person I was. Somehow, all of this has to work out for my good, doesn't it?

I want to be able to look back over my life and peruse my life's pages. I want to be proud of taking risks, not staying down and being open to new routes. My destination is set and secure. I know whatever it will be brimming with adventure and new life. I'm not scared anymore. I no longer want to be held in by the box that I now see was created by me and my version of "happily ever after." As I sit to write this, this September would have been my eighth wedding anniversary! It seems so surreal. I'm not sure exactly what to feel. Perhaps, by now we would have expanded our family to include a child...maybe two? I have no idea. As much as I would have cherished our marriage, it's over. Now, I have two choices: stay behind with what's familiar or move forward into the unknown. I had to keep moving and the only direction was up...upstream that is.

For the most part, I've moved on, and the pieces of me that straggled behind are steadily catching up. This of course, was not always the case. Some years ago, I still cried fresh tears for what could have been. I struggled to stay positive, to still have joy and to be content despite my current circumstances.

There is no magic formula to forget what life was like before your adversity forced its way into your existence. However, there is a decision to make in its aftermath. Let's discuss three realities and their potential outcomes. Of course you may not necessarily choose one of the three, you may find yourself somewhere in between. Despite your position, pay attention to characteristics of both that you may exhibit and challenge yourself to leave the middle ground.

Reality #1: The Should Have Time Capsule

Moving forward does not mean that you will never look back and wonder what "should have been," before your life was interrupted. You bundle up memories, desires and dreams and may pause for long moments in time, constantly comparing your present to your past. "I *should have* become a mother by now. "Today *should have* been his 31st birthday." "I *should have* gotten over the loss by this time." "I *should have* been in a new relationship by now." " *I should have* been healed by now." " I *should have* gotten the promotion by now." Don't get stuck in the "*should have*" time capsule. While these events may have occurred as a direct result of your storm, you have to keep moving forward in your life in order to realize your purpose and God-given dreams. If you allow yourself to get stuck, it's as if you are limiting God and telling Him that you don't believe He can do anything bigger than He has already done in your past.

It is very tempting to continue reminiscing on yesterday's good times. Fear of further exposure to uncertainty can keep you captive and stop you from moving. The comfort of safe routines that you may have experienced can almost become addicting, but don't succumb. Trust Him to go beyond your pain. Don't allow your fears of future pain limit you. Sometimes, you have so "rehearsed your misfortune," as my pastor says, that you can't be open to the newness that tomorrow brings.

Whatever took place in your past doesn't have to hold you prisoner. Use it to usher in a future that makes you savor every present moment you still have. I know that things have changed drastically, even unpleasantly. However, no one but you is stopping you from moving forward. You have to fight the natural urge to revert back to how things used to be. It is painful and uncomfortable. Sometimes, you may feel as if you are losing. I wish all I needed to do was take a deep breath, close my eyes, blink three times and exhale into a pre-trauma world where everything would be right again. Brandon would come walking through the door. At this point, I wouldn't even fuss at him for being gone so long. We would make up passionately, and my happily ever after plan would be back in full swing. Unfortunately, it doesn't work. I've tried it. I realize that no matter how many prayers I say or good thoughts I think, I can't turn back the hands of time. On the other hand, I can move forward. I must.

Reality #2: Frozen in Time

Don't let your past victories become frozen in time. The temptation to remain fixed in your past is great. The rationale is that if you don't move on, you won't have to deal with life past your pain or the memory of what has already occurred. This idea leads you to believe that you can somehow block the pain from your past and prevent it in the days to come. Unfortunately, as you continue to live, you will eventually encounter pain again and realize the reality behind your previous belief. I can relate to this on a personal level.

There was a moment when I held onto Brandon and the memory of our marriage to the point of making it my drug, my fix. Whenever things were going bad in my life or just plain didn't make sense, I would run back to the safety of my past with him. I would often reread letters, look back at old pictures of us and cry over a past that had promised me so much. I tried to make myself stay in the "oh so perfect past" instead of the harshness of my present. I think one of the real reasons we hesitate to look forward to the new things God promises to do in our lives is the fear of further pain and discomfort. We don't want to be hurt by something or someone again so we try to protect ourselves by locking the door to newness. If we truly desire to live a submitted life, we must trust that none of these events have ever or will ever take Him by surprise.

It took time, but I realized that I couldn't stay there forever. The book of Isaiah says it best, "*Do not remember the former things, neither consider the things of old, behold, I will do a new thing, and now it shall spring forth! Shall you not know it?*" You see right there, you are a given a choice to make. Will you continue to look back or will you trust Him to lead you to places that far exceed anything you could ask for or think? The emerging phase of my journey opened me up to a whole new perspective. Isn't it amazing when a shift in your perspective occurs, and you are able to look at life from a completely different vantage point? Incidents and factors that used to be minor suddenly take center stage as the pieces connect to create a totally different picture.

Looking over my own life, I slowly began to make some of these very connections as I changed my viewpoint. Instead of looking at life as something that would never yield goodness again, make the decision to approach it as a journey that can still bring something better than happiness and true joy. As with any journey, there are highs and lows. Embrace the highs and expect victory over the lows, but most importantly; keep moving. You may never know what's around the bend. Let your curiosity and "joie de vie" propel you into adventures you would have never experienced if you never took that first, fateful step.

Reality #3: Crossing Oceans

The third reality is my favorite. It is filled with unpredictable angles and experiences that pull you out of your safe cocoon and force you to take flight, much like a butterfly emerging for the first time. Due to the trauma of your exit, you tend to lose the typical shell of fear that encompasses many of those around you. You realize that you may have only one chance at this so you put everything you have into it. You allow nothing to hold you back.

I did this when I came across a unique opportunity to move abroad. Without much planning or forethought, I found myself in an uncertain place of discovery and total vulnerability. I had no idea what to do or what would come, but I welcomed the change and the freshness that it would bring into my life. With just two months of preparation, that involved: selling my house, packing up my apartment, making arrangements for my puppy, selling my car and countless checklists. In short, I moved to France.

June 29, 2013

Father, how awesome You are! I bless Your holy and beautiful name. Today I give You full honor and thank You for blessing me with this brand new day. Thank You for new life, new opportunities, and new promises! You are so faithful. God, You are my God. I lay down every burden, every task item, and wandering thought. I rejoice and I am glad, for great is my reward in You. You are real. You care about my life. You love me. You have a beautiful purpose and plan for my life. I am moving to France and wherever else You take me. My life is not mine. You are truly working everything for my good and Your glory. You will never leave me. Holy Spirit, show me what to focus on and when. Show me how to effectively multitask. I surround myself in Your presence. Take me to the next level in You Lord God. . . . I pray Your perfect will be done in every aspect of my life. Thank You for this divine connection.

In Jesus' name,

Amen

I have always loved learning new languages and absorbing different cultures, so this adventure would provide me the best of both. I was excited but nervous to say the least. I would be working as a live-in teacher of English to three boys whose knowledge of English mirrored my own understanding of French, that is to say zero, nada, null. Given all of the travel planning, my time was consumed. It left little to no time to study French. When I finally boarded the plane, the reality of my situation hit me. I remember wondering if this was the right decision. How would I make it? How would I who spoke no French, teach English to a family who didn't? This was, by far, the bravest thing I had ever done in my life. As I crossed the oceans of uncertainty, fear, doubt and anxiety; I hesitantly approached the shores of absolute trust, confidence, flexibility and sheer thrill.

September 1, 2013

I am finally sitting on the plane that will take me to the new adventure You have for me Lord. It all feels surreal, but I feel Your presence all around me. As I walked on the plane, You placed a song on my heart: "I will trust in You always, O Ancient of Days, for You are the Rock of the Ages. I will trust in You always." I feel Your peace. I am sitting next to a lovely young girl and we have connected instantly as we (try) to speak French and share the blanket Kimmy gave me. I feel great. I will not fear. The send off from the girls was so touching. Give me the words Holy Spirit to speak life, wisdom, and love. I want others to see You when they see me. Thank You for blessing me with this opportunity. Thank You for divine protection and knowledge. Increase my understanding and vocabulary, truly, put Your words in my mouth. I love You. I trust You. Lead me. I am following You.

In Jesus' name,

Amen

As I navigated my way through Charles De Gaulle, my heart raced rapidly in my chest. Was I really here? Was I really about to move in with a family that I had "spoken" to only once via Skype? I recognized the man who was here to take me to this completely new chapter in my life. Our four-hour drive from Paris to Poitiers was one of the most awkward that I can recall. Although my guide spoke English, we had no basis of familiarity, not to mention the fact that I had recently seen the movie, *Taken* (a movie filmed in Paris, whose story line presented that a young American woman had been abducted and sold into human trafficking). Therefore, taking a nap was out of the question! When we finally pulled up to the house, which resembled a mini chateau to me, I was instantly put at ease when I saw my future pupils waving a sign that welcomed me to their home: *Bienvenue Nathalie!* I don't know how to explain it, but I felt as if I already belonged, that I needed to be here at this very moment.

I was overwhelmed by the welcome I received. The French wrote the book on entertaining, and I was not disappointed. *Les apértifs* (appetizers and opening drinks) were fit for a queen. I ignorantly thought they were the main meal, until we were called *à table* (to dine). Our opening dinner of *tajine* (a Moroccan dish of chicken, rice, and lemon) remains one of my favorite dishes. The wine and cheese opened my palette to a sensory explosion I had never experienced before! The beautiful *tarte aux fruits* (fruit tart) decorated with my name on it and the musical performance put on by my young charges, opened me up to another side of the ocean that I had never imagined crossing. My private lodgings spoiled me lavishly. I quickly adapted to the positive aspects of risk-taking and plunging into the unknown.

As the months flew by, we became a family in every way. I shared my faith, language, American traditions and personal life experiences. In return, I received a plethora of recipes, true friendship, language, culture and an intimate invitation into *la mode française* (French style). We laughed at our stereotypical views of one another's cultures. We educated each other and those around us with the truth. I watched in awe as I was able to communicate my thoughts and even tell jokes in another language. The boys and their parents beamed with pride when they could speak to my American friends and be understood in English. I had risen to the challenge of newness and succeeded. We traveled all over the beautiful country of France, and I embraced it all.

Every moment was a teachable one, and I exhausted every chance I had to learn what I could. I grew in my self-belief, and I made new friends. I learned new skill sets, including driving a stick-shift minivan! I studied hard and welcomed the chance to add another language to my repertoire. I gained three little brothers and a slew of extended family. I was finally living in the present moment and seizing each day as it was given to me. When challenges arose, I applied what I had learned during one of the stormiest seasons of my life and kept swimming. I learned how to write, read, speak and mingle in a language I had never studied before taking that leap of faith in June 2013, when I said yes to this beautiful adventure.

Crossing oceans that summer transitioned me to a new level of expectation of a life not restricted by fear. I learned how to trust God absolutely and leaned on Him even more in this new land. I was seeing up close that my tragedy had not only brought pain and grief but had surprised me with a growing boldness and openness towards the unknown. These tools were invaluable and would be used continually on my life journey. I had trusted God with the uncommon and had been met with exceedingly and abundant joy, friendship, wisdom and greatness that qualified me for the next stages of a life not bound by my past. Your steps are ordered by the Creator of the Universe. Move forward with Him and trust that He knows what He's doing and where He's taking you.

Chapter 11:

Returning to Shore

I regained my ability to maneuver the surface of the water gently, yet firmly. This emerging has been the perfect balance of challenge and accomplishment. I find that I have been the most open to change and less resistant to normalcy than ever before. This was the chapter that, although mirrored the symptoms of moments I had experienced before, solidified the *"what now?"* part of my voyage.

Being the planner that I am, I had come up with multiple options as to what direction my life could go in. When I returned from France in the late summer of 2014, I had many concrete expectations of what my life should be but gradually realized that I was still not in control. Life was still not going down the path I expected. Surely, I would have met the love of my life abroad or en route to the states. I would regal my friends with our whirlwind international romance and his professions of love as I packed up my life and moved back to France. Only this time, I would settle in Paris, the world's capital of love.

Imagine my surprise when none of the above happened, and the only man I brought back with me *was on the cover of a French magazine.* I found myself in a place of confusion again. As I came down off the high my international adventure had afforded me, the question that continued to resurface was: **what now?**

In all honesty, I had no idea. I realized that crossing oceans and swimming in the deep end were all lovely metaphors, but what was I supposed to do in real life? I could no longer hide behind the shock of my tragedy, I had to face what I had been left with and embrace the uncertainty that I had so often run away from. I would have to go ashore.

I returned to the first place of my calling, the classroom; and I taught third grade after a four-year break. Talk about reality check! I had to virtually begin all over again, *again*, and frankly, I thought this was getting to be old. I thought I had shown God that He could trust with the really important and BIG assignments. Why was I back in the place where it had all started? What could I possibly learn?

My journey was truly coming full circle. As I adapted to new standards and expectations, I was stretched beyond myself. I learned how to rely on Christ in a whole new way, and minister to the individual and varied needs of each one of my students in the process. That year back in the classroom reignited my fervor to stimulate change in education through the unique vantage point of a classroom teacher. I was reminded of the things that I had committed to change and do different on behalf of fellow educators. I realized that I could have more than one purpose in life, and that I had an obligation to fulfill all of them through the second chance I had been given at life.

This portion of my trek appeared to be a detour or roadblock, determined to hinder my true calling and life purpose. I slowly learned that it was the catalyst to awakening a new mission that had been hidden inside of me all along. You may find yourself at what seems to be the end of something that you understood and could make sense of; but now, you have no idea which way to go. You've tried things in the past, but to no avail, nothing seems to last. I encourage you to take another look at your first set of instructions.

It may be that you need to revisit your last assignment. Perhaps, you never finished it. In my case, I needed to go back, not because I never completed it; but rather to offer me a new point of view. This may be the same for you. Complete your assignment; leave the details and specifics up to Him. Too often, we allow ourselves to become so wrapped up in everything else that we completely miss the point of the assignment in the first place. We become completely distracted and then question tenets that once served as the foundation of what we stood on. We have a tendency to run with a vision or dream we feel God has given us, and then we hit a roadblock when we take a moment to absorb the enormity of the assignment and the possibility of it being realized. Stay focused. Do not get distracted and caught up on the aspects of a project He created you to complete. He is completely capable. Are you then able to trust Him with as much certainty?

I love the inspirational moments in movies or live games when the underdog wins. Everyone may have spoken against that team. Sometimes fans start to leave early, having already decided who the winner and loser will be. Isn't it awesome when something shifts? A point or an impossible move is made, and suddenly, onlookers are frozen in anticipation of what comes next. Their attention is back. The unlikely has happened. They're confused. The outcome surprises everyone but the underdogs. You see, somehow.... some way.... they knew they would win. They never left the field. They pushed through the jeers, the doubting crowd and the opposing onlookers waving those towel things to distract them on the court; and they never wavered. Now I'm sure they were fearful, nervous and wondered what would happen if they failed; but they wouldn't know the verdict unless they finished the game. Finish the game. Don't walk off the playing field of life. You have teammates counting on you. You have to give it your all because if you don't, what was the point of showing up?

Approach each door of opportunity as if it were waiting on you to be opened. *"See, I have placed before you an open door that no one can shut. I know that you have little strength, yet you have kept my word and have not denied my name."* [1] Your life assignment doesn't end until you take your last breath. Don't live to die. Seize every moment as a canvas to display what you have learned and what you have discovered along your journey. Challenge yourself to keep trying your best. Dare yourself to super exceed even your own expectations.

He whispers to you... "*I'm proud of you.*" Despite the situations and people that may have tried to take you off the field and out of the game, you are still here. You are still showing up for practice, getting in your uniform and learning the plays. You are applying yourself daily the best you can, and He **is** proud of you. Often, I ask Him, "Who am I that you believe so much in me?" As I hear His answer, He fills me with an overshadowing peace that pursues me until I believe that I am everything He said I am: a victor, a daughter, a princess, a conqueror. When I look at myself through His eyes, I am amazed at what I see. I see past my flaws and brokenness, and instead see who He said I was before even one of my days came to be. Who does God say you are?

One of my memorable teaching moments occurred during the early part of my teaching tenure on career day, when I taught first grade. I recall writing the age-old self-introspection question on the board: "What do I want to be when I grow up?" Immediately little hands were raised as they shouted out the generic answers we're almost trained to say: "A firefighter!" "I want to be a doctor for animals!" "A police man!" "A lawyer!" "A teacher!" One precocious little girl, Holanda, raised her hand and said: "Una estylista." As

I wrapped my head around the uniqueness of her desire to be a stylist, she completely challenged my thinking when she further said: "But, do I have to wait 'till I grow up? I am it now." Holanda owned her desire and refused to let age, experience or perceptions tell her she would have to wait. She realized that she not only had to believe in herself, but she had to become it.

Children have what I call "fearless faith." They never consider fear as they leap into the world of possibilities before them. They're selfish in their pursuit of adventure and newness. They come up with answers to difficult questions on the spot and dare anyone to counter them. Their innocence should never be confused with ignorance, but rather sheer determination to rise above a status quo that doesn't even exist in their world. Unfortunately, these inquisitive and fearless children grow up to realize that their kind of thinking is at odds with society's system. They learn to doubt themselves. They label their once realistic dreams as fantasies. They take their place in the "real world" and leave the dreaming and hoping to artists. They face obstacles as if they were insurmountable. They forget the freedom they experienced when they thought anything was possible.

You have to try again. Do you remember the sheer determination you exhibited when you were trying to learn to do something for the first time? The rush of adrenaline and the slight shadow of fear combined to propel you forward as you only saw success in your direct line of sight. You must not let fear, tragedy, anxiety, the economy, family, friends, or foe deter you from your goal of success.

It may take you a moment to adjust back to life on land. Take your time, and apply all you've learned one day at a time. Breathe! You'll remember how life above water used to be, only this time, you'll savor every moment and try to live it the fullest.

----

[1] Revelations 3: 8 b, NIV

Chapter 12:

My Safe Harbor

I waited as long as I could. I tried to delay this book, my story. I wanted to tie a neat, pretty bow on it and right before saying: "The End," insert the classic and essential adage of every fairytale: "and they lived happily ever after."

In this case, "they" would be me and my loving, Jesus-addicted, handsome, cultured, muscular, and TALL new husband. You, the reader, would sit back with a contented sigh as you read of my life's upheaval, but do not despair, the happy ending would be in a glossy 3x5 photo on the book jacket. You would see my new husband and me and maybe even read about my new baby. I would relate to the animal lovers with a cute one-liner about my dog, Shelby. You would say to yourself, "Wow, look how God made her pain go away. He is so faithful and good. I am so happy for her. She deserves every bit of happiness, and I wish her the best." You would put the book on your bookshelf or maybe pass it on to a friend or relative going through tough times. You would encourage them to read the whole book to see how God can turn any situation around.

You might even start a book club (hint, hint ☺).

Fortunately, my conscience wouldn't let me do that to you. I have to be honest. I am still hurting. There are still days and nights that I cry until my eyes are purple. I try to talk to friends and family, but often feel that no one truly understands. I pray. I fast. I read inspirational books to keep me going, however ultimately, I always find myself at the same place: His feet. I cling to Him. I try to bargain with Him. I ask Him tough questions. I try to reason with Him. My new struggle has not been with grief or loss, but trust. I had to trust God and His way of doing things. I had to relinquish my control to His. I had to acknowledge that I was never in control.

Quite frankly, this has been a lesson of a lifetime, more than the values I learned from my short marriage to Brandon. I had to learn how to be obedient to my Maker *even when I did not want to.* I had to learn that my obedience and trust were the best gifts that I could ever give Him, not just money, time, and talents. While all of those are important in their own respect, how could any of them mean anything if I didn't wholeheartedly believe in the One who required them?

For the past six years, I have run away from this book. A typical conversation between God and me went something like this:

"Father, this is too painful! I can't do it. I don't want to!"

"My grace is sufficient for you."

"Yea, I know that Bible verse, but You don't understand. I just want to be healed and whole, once and for all. I want to be done with this pain thing!"

"In this world, you will have tribulation; but be of good cheer, I have overcome the world."

"But Daddy, haven't I suffered enough? I'm tired."

"Do not grow weary in well-doing, for in due season, you will reap, if you don't faint."

"Is it my due season yet?"

At this point, He usually cuts right to the chase, gently, but directly.

"Nathalie, you are not in control, I am. You cannot do things the way you want to, when you want to; I AM the Author of your life and love story. I know you think I broke your life beyond repair, but I am the mender of broken places. I created you. I know you are lonely, tired, frustrated, scared, and angry, but trust Me. Do as I have commanded you, even when you don't like it. I will never lead you astray. I see what

you cannot. Trust me. Stay with me. Write and be healed. Incline your ear and do what you hear me tell you to do. I love you. It hurt me to hurt you. But remember, there is not a single tear that you have ever shed that I have not caught. You are etched on the palms of my hands. I know the thoughts and plans I have for you. I know it all. I see it all. I can fix it all, and I am as you walk in obedience. Now, dry your tears and come to me."

You would think that I would have jumped right up and got back to work, but no. Similar to the Israelites who took 40 years to make a journey that could have been completed in 11 days, it took me almost 6 years to complete this book. While I don't really know how much faster I could have completed it, God in His grace, walked with me every step of the way, just like He did with the Israelites. He is patient in our stubbornness and childish antics.

It really is not over until God says it is. Even the most unpromising scenes of your story can lead to an unexpected turn in your favor. You must keep watching. Do not look away even when it is tempting to. I trust God to write my story better than I think I could? Do you?

He had broken me, absolutely crushed me. Now in the rebuilding process, I was being transformed into a completely different person. Through my sorrow and deep grief, I began to see what it truly meant to follow Christ through it all. There was nothing beautiful about my process. Frankly, it was quite ugly. It felt messy, and there was nothing neat or organized about it.

However, as life meets me daily, I have begun to realize that inexplicable euphoria tinged with peace often accompanies a period of turmoil and pain in my life. This phenomenon is what James calls, "joy." These three simple letters describes a gift that only God can give. It transcends happiness, it bypasses the "just ok" feeling, and it replaces sorrow. The words joy and challenge did not always belong together in my book of life, but the Bible plainly juxtaposes them in James 1: 2-4: "*My brethren, count it all joy when you fall into various trials, knowing that the testing of your faith produces patience. But let patience have its perfect work, that you may be perfect and complete, lacking nothing.*" The Message Bible puts it this way: "*Consider it a sheer gift, friends, when tests and challenges come at you from all sides. You know that under pressure, your faith-life is forced into the open and shows its true colors. So don't try to get out*

of anything prematurely. Let it do its work so you become
mature and well-developed, not deficient in any way."

As I walked through the valley of the shadow of
death, I heard rumors of this entity that would turn my
mourning into dancing and my tears into laughter. The
desire to encounter it for myself kept me moving. I longed
to be on the other side of pain, to remember what it was
to smile again and really mean it. I ached to experience the
bubble of laugher in the pit of my stomach. What do you do
when you're in the valley? How do you keep living when
everything inside you just wants to curl up and cry your life
away?

I don't know your individual and unique struggle,
but I do know that this "testing and trying" you're
experiencing is pushing you to a place of joy and beauty
that only the ugliness and pain of this moment could allow
you to see it. So keep pushing. Keep waking up. Try your
best. There will be days and moments in which you don't
know how you'll get out of bed or function through a day.
Rely on Him. Call on Him. Jesus hears your every cry. The
Bible says He keeps a record of your tears, even the ones
you don't let anyone see. Trust Him with your pain. He
already has a plan for it.

Looking back at that particular moment in my season made me realize that I was much stronger than I thought. But, of course, He knew that. He knew on my wedding day, when I said "till death do us part," that it would one day. He knew on the day Brandon got in his car on his way to church. He knew throughout all of the funeral preparations. He had already seen me on that February day that gathered family and friends from all over to lay to rest a man whom we all felt was just getting started. His ways and methods will never make sense to me; but if they did, He wouldn't be who He says He is. *"But what about you?" He asked. "Who do you say I am?"*[1] Who is He to you?

The aftermath of pain is joy unspeakable. Despite what you've gone through, God is faithful. He cannot lie. He is awesome in His completeness. He never leaves anything unfinished, including your life. Give Him something to work with. Show Him that He can trust you to show up and give it your all. Be of good courage, for He has overcome the world!

How amazing it is to think that the same God who formed everything we see and everything in you cares about what happens to you. He is in control. There is nothing that catches Him by surprise. Everything you've been through and will go through, anything you've done and will do is already known by our Father. He loves you.

This process is what the Lord has you experience in order to learn something about yourself. It forces you to focus on a specific area or issue that will stretch you willingly or unwillingly. I look back at Moses in the Holy Scriptures. He was minding his own business, living in comfort, blind to the war going on for his soul. He was a good person. He cared about the well being of his fellow neighbors. I often wondered if he missed the comfort of his former life. That life had virtually no surprises. His life was pretty much mapped out for him. He grew up in the palace and was sheltered from the hardships that his unknowing fellow family members shared. Then God interrupted his life. His true life began after that interruption.

I believe the same happens in our lives. In the end, through time and a loss of self reliance and direction, you learn how to trust Him even when your feet can't touch bottom.

\----------------------

[1] Matthew 16:15

Notes

[i.] immerse. (n.d.). Dictionary.com Unabridged.
Retrieved January 13, 2016 from Dictionary.com website
http://dictionary.reference.com/browse/immerse

[ii.] James 1: 2-4 NKJV

[iii.] Acts 26:2a NKJV

[iv.] Matthew 26:39 NIV

[v.] Taken from the Book of Common Prayer

[vi.] submerge. (n.d.). Dictionary.com Unabridged.
Retrieved January 13, 2016 from Dictionary.com
websitehttp://dictionary.reference.com/browse/
submerge

[vii.] Romans 8:28 NIV

[viii.] Habakkuk 2: 2,3 NIV

[ix.] Philippians 3:13,14 The Message Bible

[x.] (Reference Genesis 32:30)

[xi.] Isaiah 45:3 NIV

[xii] Job 13:15, 16 NIV

[xiii.] Song of Solomon 3:4, NKJV

[xiv.] emerge. (n.d.). Dictionary.com Unabridged.
Retrieved January 13, 2016 from Dictionary.com website
http://dictionary.reference.com/browse/emerge

[xv.] Revelations 3: 8 b, NIV

[xvi.] Matthew 16:15